BODY, SOUL

and

SPIRIT

BODY, SOUL
and
SPIRIT

J. Carter Swaim

THOMAS NELSON & SONS

EDINBURGH   NEW YORK   TORONTO

Library of Congress Catalogue Card Number: 57-14968

TO
BILL
AND
BOB

Table of Contents

III. SPIRIT

Preface

Many circumstances made this book inevitable. Medicine has discovered that anger can do as much damage to the body as bacteria, that loss of a limb and loss of a loved one may be equally traumatic, and that we sometimes eat too much because we do not get on well with others. Bacteria, shattered limbs, and diet are the concern of medicine. But anger, sorrow, and loneliness are plainly in the sphere of religion.

Rediscovery of the relationship between medicine and religion comes at a time when the resources of religion are available as they have not been for generations. New discoveries in the realm of Biblical knowledge are quite as significant for the life of man as anything that has come out of scientific laboratories.

The finding of ancient manuscripts has at many important points corrected our understanding of the truth God spoke long ago. Fresh translation enables us to discover meaning where before there was only perplexity. Gratitude is expressed to the National Council of Churches for permission to use the REVISED STANDARD VERSION OF THE HOLY BIBLE.

The Dead Sea Scrolls have served to accentuate certain truths found in the canonical Scripture. The Apocrypha, regarded as canonical in parts of Christendom, have also been newly translated by the Standard Bible Committee. Both these sources have been laid under tribute in the present work.

Dr. Russell Dicks, professor of pastoral care at the Divinity School of Duke University, first suggested that the time was ripe for a fresh study of Scripture and Health. Some sections of this book appeared as articles in *Religion and Health*, the monthly magazine edited by Dr. Dicks. Doctors used to report that, of all the magazines in their waiting rooms, *Religion and Health* was the one most often stolen!

The organizational plan of the book is derived from I Thess. 5.23, except that the words have been taken in inverse order. Where Paul writes "spirit and soul and body," we have dealt successively with body, soul, and spirit. Within the three main sections of the book, the several studies are arranged in what seems to the author a logical sequence. Each unit, however, is self-contained and may be read without reference to the rest.

"Body" treats of those portions of the Scripture which deal with physical well-being. Concerning God's commandment Moses said to the people: "It is not in heaven, that you should say, 'Who will go up for us to heaven, and bring it to us, that we may hear it and do it?' Neither is it beyond the sea, that you should say, 'Who will go over the sea for us, and bring it to us, that we may hear it and do it?' But the word is very near you; it is in your mouth and in your heart, so that you can do it" (Deut. 30.12-14).

The Scripture shows how God has brought healing down to earth. We are his workmanship (Eph. 2.10), and the rainbow is the sign and pledge of "the everlasting covenant between God and every living creature of all flesh that is upon the earth" (Gen. 9.16). God has provided food to

sustain us—but we do not live to eat. Water and medicine
and laughter have their part to play in the healing of the
body. Nurses and physicians are his ministers to our need.
There is stern Scriptural warning against those who abuse
the God-given faculties of healing.

"Soul" treats of those impulses which are within us all,
and calls attention to Scripture passages which help with
self-discipline and the management of anger and anxiety;
with the peace that comes from believing the right things
about God; with the meaning of salvation and the significance of togetherness. Francis of Assisi spoke of the body as
"our brother the ass." Mind and emotion must be so managed as not to cause this brother to misbehave.

"If any one is in Christ," says Paul (2 Cor. 5.17), "he is a
new creation." "Spirit" treats of those higher reaches of experience which come to us through God's extra gifts of hope
and love, of peace and gratitude, of imaginative sympathy.
These serve to put pain and suffering in a light not easily
comprehended by body or soul.

Medical information contained herein is not derived from
a professional study of medicine but is only such as is readily
available to the layman. It has no other authority than that
of reports that can be seen in any public library.

It remains only to thank Oscar W. Brooks for his patience
in deciphering my handwriting, his skill in preparing the
manuscript, and his willing co-operation at every point.

J. CARTER SWAIM

I. BODY

1. The Bible and Our Diseases

A surgeon has recently suggested that, for some aspects of their work, medical students may receive more help in the Bible than in the laboratory. Dr. Allen O. Whipple, professor emeritus of surgery at Columbia University's College of Physicians and Surgeons, has urged young practitioners to give "special attention to human behavior patterns portrayed in great plays, biographies, and historical works." He insists that "more is to be learned from the stories of Moses, Isaac, Joseph, Job, David, and Hosea, than by studying mice in a maze."

Looking back upon fifty years of dealing with human problems in a career that has brought him into touch with the leading men of his profession, a psychiatrist says: "If you were to take the sum total of all the authoritative articles ever written by the most qualified of psychologists and psychiatrists on the subject of mental hygiene—if you were to combine them and refine them and clean out the excess verbiage—if you were to take the whole of the meat and none of the parsley, and if you were to have these unadulterated bits of pure scientific knowledge concisely expressed by the most capable of living poets, you would have an awkward and incomplete summary of the Sermon on the Mount."

Churchmen, on the other hand, have felt that their ministrations were incomplete apart from co-operation with members of the medical profession. The Church of England set up a Commission on Divine Healing, and requested the

3

co-operation of the British Medical Association in collecting data which would help to determine whether unexplained recoveries from prolonged illness were due to "suggestion, spontaneous remission, or Divine intervention." Doctors who had had experiences involving unexplained cures were asked to report whether the patients' recovery was attended by spiritual ministrations; if so, whether these had taken the form of healing services, the laying on of hands, or anointing with oil. They were asked also to indicate whether such experiences as public or private prayer or pilgrimages to such places as Lourdes were involved.

The doctors subsequently reported that there was considerable evidence that religious ministrations were of value in the treatment of various disorders, but no evidence that "spiritual healing" could be effective apart from medical means. Declaring that there was a sense in which all healing could be thought of as divine, the Committee went on to say that "many aspects of healing are still outside our present knowledge and this we should honestly and humbly admit."

If religion and medicine are now joining hands for the benefit of man, that is simply a bringing together of two phases of life which ought never to have been separated. The discovery that religion has something to do with health is one the twentieth century thinks is peculiarly its own. But it was widely practiced in the middle ages—and had to be if men were to follow the example of Christ and the healing mission of the apostles. The church and the hospital were one and the same. The porches of the bishops' houses were in very early times utilized to care for the sick poor. These were in fact, the only havens open to those ill in body and mind. It was the church which preserved the medical lore of the Greeks. Monastic orders built penitentiaries and hospitals. Some of these latter "were built like a cruciform church with the chancel for a chapel, the transepts for the beds of the patients and a short nave for the living quarters of the members of the religious order who tended the sick."

Clergymen of a later age were interested in the sum total of human behavior. Jonathan Edwards is best known for his sermon "Sinners in the Hands of an Angry God," but that sermon was not characteristic of his ministry. Edwards was a scientist who always wanted to know why things were as they were. As a child he crammed his notebook with interrogations: "Why, having two eyes, do we not see double?" "To show why distant mountains are blue," "to know the shape of the spheroid of the universe by observation of the milky way." He made careful observations regarding his own manner of life. "I think I find myself more sprightly and healthy both in body and mind," he wrote, "for my self-denial in eating, drinking, and sleeping." He was keenly interested in his own inner world, and undertook to analyze his dreams in order to discover "what are the nature, circumstances, principles, and ends of my imaginary actions and passions in them."

If this sounds strangely like psychoanalysis, it has to be said that it was his concern about the truths of the Bible which led Edwards into all such observation. Preachers in years gone by had not our modern knowledge of psychiatry, but their ministry was effective in the cure of souls because they knew their Bibles. Commenting on *Master Sermons of the Nineteenth Century,* Gaius Glenn Atkins points out that they "lack the modern psychological techniques but they know human nature and touch its faults and failures with uncanny insight."

One of Edwards' major concerns was the writing of his "Treatise Concerning the Religious Affections." His "Narrative of Surprising Conversions" reveals how the New England citizens of that day were impelled by religion to a better relation with their neighbors. "Never, I believe," he wrote, "was so much done in confessing injuries and making up of differences . . . People had done with their old quarrels, back-bitings, and intermeddling with other men's matters." If this sounds like the kind of happy "adjustment" for which the psychiatrist seeks, it must be remembered that Edwards and his converts based it upon the Scripture.

Edwards wrote this definition of religion: "The essence of all true religion lies in holy love; and in this divine affection and an habitual disposition to it and that light which is the foundation of it and those things which are the fruits of it, consists the whole of religion." It is not a far cry from that to the form of prescription sometimes used at a modern psychiatric clinic: "Two weeks of unsolicited love." That is to say, doctors and nurses are to bestow upon the patient that full measure of brotherly love which the patient needs but does not know how to ask for.

Two books of the New Testament were written by a medical man. Concerning the author of our third Gospel, Paul writes of "Luke the beloved physician." The Acts of the Apostles is a second volume by the same author. Eusebius of Caesarea, who has been called the father of church history, in describing Luke's contribution to Christian literature, says that he "having associated mainly with Paul and having companied with the rest of the apostles less closely, has in two inspired books left us examples of that healing of souls which he acquired from them." The doctor's careful capacity for observation is apparent both in the Gospels and in Acts. Matthew (12.10) and Mark (1.1) tell how Jesus in the synagogue encountered a man "with a withered hand." The more clinically minded Luke, however, reports, "a man was there whose right hand was withered" (Luke 6.6). Acts 3.7 sounds like a medical report: "And he took him by the right hand and raised him up; and immediately his feet and ankles were made strong."

Mark 5.25ff tells of a woman who for twelve years had been having hemorrhages. She "had suffered much under many physicians, and had spent all that she had, and was no better but rather grew worse." Luke, too, tells about this patient with a prolonged affliction, and in the King James Bible relates that she "had spent all her living upon physicians." Note, however, that this comment does not occur in RSV because it is not found in the best Greek texts. They simply relate that she "could not be healed by any one" (Luke 8.43). In other words, here is Dr. Luke preserving the good name of the medical profession. He does not blame her chronic illness upon the incompetence of his colleagues but rather upon the woman herself; the poor creature just did not have the strength to get well!

Better translation at several points makes it clear that Luke the physician is speaking. At Luke 4.38 the King James Version says "Simon's wife's mother was taken with a great fever." The word translated "great," however, is a technical medical term, and the REVISED STANDARD VERSION rightly renders the passage, "Now Simon's mother-in-law was ill with a high fever." Acts 28.8 in the King James, says that "the father of Publius lay sick of a fever, and of a bloody flux." The REVISED STANDARD VERSION gives a more specific diagnosis: "The father of Publius lay sick with fever and dysentery." Luke 5.18, in the King James, tells how "men brought in a bed a man which was taken with a palsy." The Greek word here is a technical one describing loss of power in the lower limbs. The REVISED STANDARD translates, "men were bringing on a bed a man who was paralyzed." The English word "palsy" is a corruption of the French *paralysie*.

A better translation at Matthew 17.15 reflects not only a changed world view but is infinitely kinder to a group of the afflicted in our society. The King James Version here says: "Lord, have mercy on my son; for he is lunatic, and sore vexed: for oftimes he falleth into the fire, and oft into the water." The REVISED STANDARD here reads: "Lord, have mercy on my son, for he is an epileptic and he suffers terribly; for often he falls into the fire, and often into the water." The symptoms are plainly those of epilepsy, and it is right that our English rendering should name the disease. The parallel passage in Mark 9.18 gives an even more detailed description of the convulsion: "It dashes him down; and he foams and grinds his teeth and becomes rigid."

The Greek word which the King James translates "lunatic" originally meant "moonstruck." Primitive man believed that there was a connection between epilepsy and the phases of the moon. One old churchman who challenged this belief was informed that madness was not really caused by the moon but by the devil who avails himself of the moonlight for his work. "Lunatic" is a term that has now come to mean "A person whose abnormal mental condition renders him incapable or irresponsible before the law." This is plainly not what Matthew was describing, and it is unfair and inaccurate to imply that epilepsy necessarily means lessening of mental power. The English term "epilepsy" is itself a curious survival of an old belief. The word is Greek for "seized upon," and assumes that one thus possessed has fallen under the power of evil spirits; this is preserved in our "seizure."

It is interesting to note in this connection that one of the New Testament words for illness has had a curious rebirth in modern times. The Greek word asthenia means "want of strength, weakness, illness." It occurs in the plural in Acts 28.9 and is translated "diseases." In 1 Timothy 5.23 the King James translates it "infirmities," the REVISED STANDARD "ailments." A. J. Cronin, British doctor, novelist, and autobiographer, invented for the wealthy people of Mayfair who thought it fashionable to go to expensive physicians, even when they had no disease, an ailment which he called "asthenia." His patients were unaware that it simply meant weakness or debility, and soon his anti-asthenia injections were the toast of the town. "Again and yet again," he says, "my sharp and shining needle sank into fashionable buttocks, bared upon the finest linen sheets. I became expert, indeed superlative, in the art of penetrating the worst end of the best society."

In St. Luke's bay at the New York cathedral, the cusps surrounding the medallions where the miracles of Christ are pictured show the figures of four medical men: Pasteur, who introduced the control of bacteria by pasteurization; Lister, the first to practice antiseptic surgery; Hippocrates, the ancient Greek physician whose oath for the medical profession is still used when young men are admitted to the healing art; and the country doctor. The interlarding of these figures with Christ's work is intended to reveal the wholeness of man and the need for religion and science to join hands for his well-being. The Scripture makes it clear that this was so among the people through whom God revealed Himself long ago.

2. Religion and Health

When New York City's health department was established, the Commissioners in their first annual report deplored the fact that the great metropolis had paid so little attention to the conditions under which the citizens might live out their lives in health. "This is a remarkable fact," they said, "considering the antiquity of the Mosaic Code, the greatest collection of health laws ever published." It is notable that the

Mosaic Code, found in the Old Testament, envisioned a close relation between religion and health. The only health officers, in fact, were those who also led in the temple worship. Deuteronomy 21.5 tells us of the priests, "the LORD your God has chosen them to minister to him and to bless in the name of the LORD, and by their word every dispute and every assault shall be settled." So also to the priests, as civil officers of the community, was entrusted the administration of regulations regarding health.

Leviticus is the book which describes the duties of the priests. Its name is derived from the tribe of Levi, whose sons were entrusted with the priesthood. A section of the book (chapters 11 to 15), sets forth regulations regarding the conduct of the priests as they were charged with preserving the health of the community. It has been said that these chapters "are perhaps the least attractive in the whole Bible." From the point of view of anthropology they seem to be made up of primitive taboos. From the point of view of sociology, they reflect practices that may seem unnecessarily harsh and cruel. From the point of view of medicine, they have little to offer the modern practitioner. Admittedly, too, their language is not our language. The fact is, however, that their problems are our problems, and it is suggestive to study how God's people in ancient times dealt with situations which still perplex.

A number of medical terms used in the REVISED STANDARD VERSION of this passage are more in keeping with modern technical knowledge than the terms of the King James. Leviticus 13.30 gives directions for diagnosing what KJV calls "a dry scall." RSV calls it "an itch." Leviticus 13.39, KJV, refers to "a freckled spot that groweth in the skin." "Freckle" there seems to be used in the sense of scab. A freckle is now a bit of brown pigmentation which may lend sauciness to the face of a small boy or charm to a young girl. The REVISED

STANDARD VERSION here reads: "It is tetter that has broken out in the skin." Tetter is defined as "any of various vesicular skin diseases, as ringworm, eczema, and herpes." Irregular sexual practices, disguised in KJV as "confusion" (Lev. 18.23), are in RSV frankly and accurately called "perversion."

Since religion, government, and medical care were all a common concern, the Scripture provides certain diagnostic regulations to guide the priests. In the detection of that large number of afflictions covered by the term "leprosy," a change in the color of the hair was held to be an important symptom. Jet black hair was generally characteristic of the tribe, but infection might alter this in various parts of the body. A sore spot which "appears no deeper than the skin, and the hair in it has not turned white" (Lev. 13.4) was not considered serious. On the other hand, "if there is a white swelling in the skin, which has turned the hair white" (Lev. 13.10), drastic treatment is required. Again, in the case of difficulty with the scalp or beard, "if it appears deeper than the skin, and the hair in it is yellow and thin" (Lev. 13.30), another diagnosis is indicated.

Quarantine is a term now used for the temporary isolation of persons who are either suffering from communicable disease or have been exposed to it. The term, derived from the Latin and indicating a period of forty days, seems to have originated in the twelfth century in Venice, where incoming ships were required to wait offshore for forty days. Until 1937, New York harbor required all vessels to anchor at "Quarantine"—a U. S. Public Health station located on the Staten Island bank of the Narrows—and undergo inspection by medical officers. Now, however, the word of the ship's physician is accepted. The Hebrew medical code also provided for quarantine. If diagnosis of suspicious signs has not been completed, "the priest shall shut up the diseased person for seven days" (Lev. 13.4;cf 13.26, 31). If the symptoms continue but not too pronouncedly, "the priest shall shut up the person with the itching disease for seven days more" (Lev. 13.33). Isolation of contagious disease is enjoined in Numbers 5.1: "The Lord said to Moses, 'Command the people of Israel that they put out of the camp every leper, and every one having a discharge.'"

Americans now in middle life can recall when fumigation was practiced. This process of "disinfection by means of noxious fumes derived from formaldehyde or sulphur" was formerly considered necessary if rooms which had housed persons with communicable disease were again to be habitable. Fresh air, sunlight, and thorough scrubbing of walls and contents are now deemed more effective. Where disease is suspected, scrubbing with disinfectants is still recommended for kitchen equipment, table service, and bathroom fixtures. Leviticus 14.40f described a cruder and more cumbersome process evidently intended to secure a similar result: "The priest shall command that they take out the stones in which is the disease and throw them into an unclean place outside the city; and he shall cause the inside of the house to be scraped round about."

Until fairly recently in American life, cuspidors were found in hotel lobbies, railway stations, and many living rooms. The plushier resorts were distinguished, not by the absence of cuspidors, but rather by the size and shininess of their brass spittoons. "Spitting Prohibited" signs are still to be seen in public conveyances. The reason is sometimes given: "spitting spreads disease." The Hebrews knew this, too, and provided that "if he who has the discharge spits on one who is clean, then he shall wash his clothes, and bathe himself in water, and be unclean until the evening" (Lev. 15.8). Provision is also made for disinfecting beds (Lev. 15.4) and saddles (Lev. 15.9) that may have been contaminated by infection. "And the earthen vessel which he who has the discharge touches shall be broken; and every vessel of wood shall be rinsed in water" (Lev. 15.12).

American communities have regulations regarding reportable diseases. A doctor who sees patients with highly communicable infections is required to notify the local health authorities. Under certain circumstances something of this kind was required also in ancient Israel. Leviticus 14.35 states that when there is reason to believe that a house is infected, "then he who owns the house shall come and tell the priest, 'There seems to me to be some sort of disease in my house.'"

Westerners are apt to consider that the worst thing about caste-ridden countries is that the pariah class must keep out of the way of other classes. Equally cruel appears the banishment imposed upon lepers: "He shall wear torn clothes and let the hair of his head hang loose, and he shall cover his upper lip and cry, 'Unclean, unclean' ... he shall dwell alone in a habitation outside the camp" (Lev. 13.45f). In other words, he was to dress like a mourner, with frayed clothes and unkempt hair. The beard, of which the Oriental was proud, was to be veiled. The victim must be kept from association with the ordinary populace. If this seems cruel, we must rather remind ourselves that the priests were actually using what seemed then the necessary method for preventing the spread of contagion. Every modern hospital has its isolation ward, and every large center of population its isolation hospital.

We have said that these chapters are hardly comparable to what would be found in present-day textbooks. The section, however, has been called "The dedication of national life." It dramatizes what is implicit throughout the Scripture, namely, that religion can never be regarded as a separate compartment of life. The physical well-being of the community, the treatment of neighbors, the worship of God's house are equally its concern. Another way of saying this is that for the Hebrews religion was never simply a matter of mystical experience or private enjoyment. It had to find expression in the life of the community.

The provision that public health should be a concern of the religious authorities was not abrogated by our Lord. To the leper whom he had cleansed Jesus said: "go and show yourself to the priest, and make an offering for your cleansing, as Moses commanded, for a proof to the people" (Luke 5.14; Mt. 8.14; Mark 1.44).

The "offering for your cleansing," prescribed by Moses and recommended by Jesus (Luke 5.14), is interesting. "Two living clean birds" were to be obtained (Lev. 14.4). One of the birds was to be offered as a sacrifice, and its blood sprinkled "seven times upon him who is to be cleansed" (Lev. 14.7). The seven times was no doubt intended to suggest the completeness of the cure, just as Naaman was required to bathe seven times in the Jordan in order for healing to be effected (2 Kings 5.10, 14). Then, "he shall let the living bird go into the open field" (Lev. 14.7).

We in the twentieth century are apt to dismiss the latter as a curious survival of primitive magic, comparable to Azazel, the scapegoat. Leviticus 16.21 f provides that in the ritual of atonement the priest "shall lay both his hands upon the head of the live goat, and confess over him all the iniquities of the people . . . and he shall put them upon the head of the goat, and send him away into the wilderness . . . The goat shall bear all their iniquities upon him to a solitary land." Whatever the origin of this strange custom, it undoubtedly had great therapeutic value. Concerning God's forgiving love Psalm 103.12 says:

> "As far as the east is from the west,
>   so far does he remove our transgressions
>   from us."

But those who watched the goat disappear could see their sins being taken off to a place remote and unknown where they would never trouble them again. A similar technique is still employed in youth conferences. In moments of high commitment young people write on a piece of paper the name of some sin or weakness over which they wish to gain the victory. All present then march around the campfire and toss these pieces of paper into the flame, symbolizing the fact that these hateful things are being for ever put out of one's life. Nobody thinks there is anything magical or superstitious about this. It is rather symbolic and sacramental: an outward and visible sign of an inner and invisible change. Moreover, the performance of the outward act tends to clinch the inward resolve.

So with the bird that was released "into the open field." For the cleansed man it was not a magical but a sacramental act. It symbolized many things. The bird would quickly escape out of sight. So the man's previous isolation and unacceptability were carried away into the unknown. The bird, once captured and held in bondage, was now free to roam wherever it wanted. The patient, formerly separated from others by his disease, was now freed of restraints and able to go where he liked. The church has always considered baptism as a symbol of the washing away of sin. Perhaps Christians of the twentieth century need to develop other symbolic acts, so that the healed man may feel himself given a new lease on life, like a bird released from a cage. The Scripture makes it clear that matter was intended to serve the eternal purpose of God.

3. God Created Man

Man is a created being. In Romans 4.17 Paul speaks of God as He who "calls into existence the things that do not exist." The early chapters of Genesis represent God as successively calling into existence a universe, with an earth containing sea and land; "the great sea monsters and every living creature that moves" (Gen. 1.21) ... "and man" (Gen. 1.27). These statements are intended to be neither philosophic nor scientific. If they suggest that God created "out of nothing," philosophers will insist that this sounds as if "nothing" were a kind of negative substance out of which "something" could be formed. Others will affirm that for the phrase "out of nothing" should be substituted "without use of pre-existing materials." Arguments of this kind intrigue those of us in the western world who are the heirs of Aristotle.

They are, however, arguments that never would have occurred to the men of the Bible. Nor do the Genesis stories contain a scientific analysis of the process by which God brought these into being. Time was when well-meaning apologists for Christianity found in the evolutionary theory a parallel to the successive stages of creation found in Genesis. Land animals, for example, are represented in Genesis (1.20-25) as coming after sea animals. Since biology teaches that life began in the water and the transition to life on the land was accomplished by amphibians, we are told that this establishes that there is no conflict between Genesis and Darwin. Interesting and suggestive as this may be, it is on the wrong track. The Bible has no biology, no geology, no chemistry. It is solely a book of religion.

The Genesis stories make a religious affirmation about man. Time was when he did not exist, and God brought him into existence. Genesis (2.7) tells us that "the LORD God formed man of dust from the ground, and breathed into his nostrils the breath of life; and man became a living being." There have been those to ridicule this, as if God were simply employed in making mud pies. The religious truth—which, incidentally, turns out also to be scientific truth—here set forth is that man is fashioned out of the same elements as the earth. As the New Testament puts it, "The first man was from the earth, a man of dust" (1 Cor. 15.47).

Of all this, each funeral service is solemn reminder. The words of committal are: "earth to earth, ashes to ashes, dust to dust." Cremation provides even quicker return to the elements. Christian Science has no doctrine of creation, and so cannot recognize that earthly bodies may represent the creative activity of the Divine. Mary Baker Eddy discusses this with some frequency. "If God is Spirit, and God is All," she says, "surely there can be no matter; for the divine All must be spirit." "God is All, and God is Spirit; therefore there is nothing but Spirit; and consequently there is no matter." "I believe in matter only as I believe in evil, that it is something to be denied and destroyed to human consciousness, and is unknown to the Divine."

This would appear to be a doctrine of pantheism. Yet, says Mrs. Eddy, "We should watch and pray that we enter not into the temptation of pantheistic belief in matter as sensible mind. We should subjugate it as Jesus did, by a dominant understanding of Spirit."

The Genesis story represents woman as having been taken out of man's side: "the LORD God caused a deep sleep to fall upon the man and while he slept took one of his ribs and closed up its place with flesh; and the rib which the LORD God had taken from the man he made into a woman and brought her to the man" (Gen. 2.21f). This, too, has been ridiculed as childish. The true significance of the story is found in the preface. The ancient writer explains that God caused the animals to pass before Adam and he gave names to them, but none of them seemed a really suitable companion. God said, "It is not good that the man should be alone; I will make him a helper fit for him" (Gen. 2.18). This is the purpose for which woman was created. An old commentator observed that God did not take woman out of man's head, that she should lord it over him; nor yet out of his feet that he should trample upon her; but out of his side, that she might stand by him and be his companion. This is celebrated by Adam in the earliest hymn of thanksgiving:

> "This at last is bone of my bones
> and flesh of my flesh" (Gen. 2.23).

The significance of all this Christian Science seems also to miss. Regarding the sleep into which God graciously caused Adam to fall before operating on his side and removing his rib, Mrs. Eddy describes it as a time "when the spiritual senses were hushed by material sense that before had claimed audience with a serpent." (In Genesis, of course, it is after the woman is created that the encounter with the serpent occurs.) Mrs. Eddy seems also not to believe in the equality of men and women but to give the superior place to woman. "Man is the generic term for all humanity," she writes. "Woman is the highest species of man, and this word is the generic term for all women." One of her followers writes of woman: "Hers is the mission of missions—the highest of all— to make the body not the prison, but the palace of the soul, with the brain for its great white throne."

The wonder of God's creation as applied to our race is set forth in the Genesis stories. In Psalm 139.13-16 God is addressed as the creator of each individual:

"For thou didst form my inward parts,
> thou didst knit me together in my
>> mother's womb.
I praise thee, for thou art fearful and wonderful.
> Wonderful are thy works!
Thou knowest me right well;
> my frame was not hidden from thee,
when I was being made in secret,
> intricately wrought in the depths of the earth.
Thy eyes beheld my unformed substance;
> in thy book were written, every one of them,
the days that were formed for me,
> when as yet there was none of them."

The Psalmist did not know what we know about the science of embryology, yet he is sure the child growing in the mother's body is also an illustration of God's care for His creatures. The REVISED STANDARD VERSION helps us in almost every line of this passage. The opening phrases in the King James are: "For thou has possessed my reins: thou hast covered me in my mother's womb." "Reins," used now to describe bit and bridle, was a seventeenth-century word for kidneys. Neither seems in point here—and God does much more than "cover" us in the womb. The REVISED STANDARD VERSION enables us to understand what the Psalmist was really getting at:

"For thou didst form my inward parts,
> thou didst knit me together in my mother's womb."

The concluding lines in the King James read: "Thine eyes did see my substance, yet being unperfect; and in thy book all *my members* were written, *which* in continuance were fashioned, when *as yet there was* none of them." The large number of words in italics, terms inserted by the translators, suggests how inadequately these phrases were understood in the seventeenth century. The REVISED STANDARD VERSION indicates God's concern for the developing embryo and the days unfolding before it:

> "Thy eyes beheld my unformed substance;
>   in thy book were written, every one of them,
>   the days that were formed for me,
>   when as yet there was none of them."

There is much which modern science still does not know about the embryo. It does not know precisely how long it takes the single cell to develop into an infant ready to breathe. And when the foetus is ready to come into the world, science does not know what initiates the process of birth. And sometimes when the new human being comes into the outer world the process of breathing does not immediately get under way, and the attending physician may have to put his mouth to the child's mouth and force air into the lungs. One of the most thrilling incidents in A. J. Cronin's novel, *The Citadel,* is of this nature. The local practitioner discards a newborn baby as destined never to live. But Andrew, skilled in obstetrics and determined to do everything within his power, is able to revive the child and make a home happy. The doctor who forces his own breath into the child in order to start its respiratory organs to functioning is very like God, of whom it is said in Genesis, "the LORD God formed man . . . and breathed into his nostrils the breath of life" (Gen. 2.7).

At his birth it is disclosed how helpless a creature man is. When he comes into the world he is farther from maturity than any other living being. A fish will be mature in a few weeks, a chicken in a few months, a dog in a few years. It is said that one year in the life of a dog is equal to seven years in the life of a man. A dog of two would be comparable to a lad of 14, and a dog of 10 to a man of 70. The creature that is man requires to be sheltered and nurtured and provided for by others for many years. Twenty-one is the number of

twelvemonth periods recognized as that required to bring
him from birth to maturity. At 21 he can vote and hold property and legally act without reference to his parents. (A boy,
however, does not have to wait that long to die for his
country. A nation which will not bestow citizenship until 21
is perfectly willing to let a lad be slaughtered at 18).

By every physical standard it would therefore be supposed
that so fragile a bundle of life would, in a universe like this,
be exactly nowhere. A hunter complains that "No other animal is put together as poorly as man." He reminds us that
man cannot swim like the otter or climb like the cat or perch
like the chimpanzee. It might also be pointed out that he is
not so agile as the panther, so swift as the rabbit, so strong as
the ox. But this does not prove man's insignificance. The
Hebrews long ago observed that "under the sun the race is
not to the swift, nor the battle to the strong" (Eccles. 9.11).

Man is a created being. God is the Creator, man the creature. Some contemporary theologies are fond of emphasizing
what a distance this sets between man and his Maker. God is
Wholly Other, we are told, and the only thing frail man can
do is bow in humble acknowledgment of his finitude. This,
however, is not the Scriptural teaching. The Bible does not
make the distinction we are prone to make between the Creator God and the Father God. It represents them as one and
the same, and the latter relationship as arising out of the
former. Isaiah 40.28f asks:

"Have you not known? Have you not heard?
    The LORD is the everlasting God,
        the Creator of the ends of the earth.

He gives power to the faint,
    and to him who has no might he increases strength."

I Peter 4.19 says: "Let those who suffer according to God's
will do right and entrust their souls to a faithful creator."

They whose "days are swifter than a weaver's shuttle" (Job 7.6) can hardly do otherwise! Man's years on earth are numbered!

4. Man Is Mortal

All men are mortal. Socrates is a man. Therefore Socrates is mortal. This is the college boy's first lesson in logic. The three statements, taken together, form a syllogism. This type of argument, meaning "reasoning together," tells us that from a major premise ("All men are mortal") and a minor premise ("Socrates is a man"), an indisputable conclusion must follow ("Socrates is mortal").

But the major premise of this syllogism is more than merely the first step in learning to use the process of valid inference. It is a universal proposition which many cultists ignore. The religion of healthy-mindness can flourish among us only as we accept the fact that "all men are mortal." That is to say, they live in bodies that are not only subject to death but are bound to die.

The tenements in which we dwell are described in Job (4.19f) as

"houses of clay,
whose foundation is in the dust,
who are crushed before the moth.
Between morning and evening they are destroyed."

Man's house is not only built upon the dust but is made of dust. It is so frail a moth can knock it over. It may perish in a single day. The hymn writer's line sums up our plight:

"Frail children of dust and feeble as frail."

Its author, Sir Robert Grant, was a statesman, scholar, and philanthropist who had many of the honors which the world can confer. He was a member of Parliament at the age of 29. He later became a privy councilor, and governor of Bombay. His philanthropies were symbolized by a medical college bearing his name in India. Yet he could not live for ever, and died at the age of 59.

The impermanence of our bodies is suggested by other figures of speech used in the Scripture. Longfellow sings of how, when "The Day Is Done,"

> "the cares that infest the day,
> Shall fold their tents, like the Arabs,
> And as silently steal away."

The tent is a Biblical symbol of transiency. In Genesis (4.20) Jabal is described as "the father of those who dwell in tents" —that is to say, lead a nomadic life.

The Rechabites, a reforming group in Israel sent to protest current evils, were not to settle down in the existing order: "you shall not build a house; you shall not sow seed; you shall not plant or have a vineyard; but you shall live in tents all your days" (Jer. 35.7). Job (4.21) says of human beings:

> "If their tent-cord is plucked up within them,
> do they not die?"

The place of worship which the Hebrews had during the wilderness wanderings was a tent. The King James Version translated the word as "tabernacle," a Latin term literally meaning "small hut." The Mormon Tabernacle in Salt Lake City has given quite other ideas about a tabernacle. The Hebrews worshiped in a wooden framework covered with curtains, and tent is the word which the REVISED STANDARD VERSION uses. Paul writes to the Corinthians: "while we are still in this tent, we sigh with anxiety" (2 Cor. 5.4).

This means that we must accept the fact that our bodies are subject to deterioration, death, and decay. We must not expect that all our diseases can be cured. A middle-aged minister reports that he was called to the bedside of his 79-year old father, whose earthly life was about to come to its close. Some organs of his body were worn out, and were gradually ceasing to function. It was clear that he was not long for this world. Yet the son learned that his sisters had been sending money to a faith-healer in a distant city, with the expectation that he would reverse the process of disintegration which had set in and restore their father to health and vigor.

The Scripture occasionally tells of a blind man who receives his sight. More often, however, we hear of failing vision due to advancing age. Genesis (27.1ff) relates an incident that occurred "When Isaac was old and his eyes were dim so that he could not see." Of the patriarch Jacob we read: "Now the eyes of Israel were dim with age, so that he could not see" (Gen. 48.10). Of the priest at Shiloh it is recorded: "Now Eli was ninety-eight years old and his eyes were set, so that he could not see" (1 Samuel 4.15). Modern optical science could probably have helped all these to see better, but the fact is the Bible records no miracle that turned back the years. David's name was great in the annals of the nation, but he too was subject to the infirmities of increasing age. The first book of Kings begins with the words, "Now King David was old and advanced in years; and although they covered him with clothes, he could not get warm" (1 Kings 1.1).

The Scripture reports many persons who were cured of their infirmity. But not even in the Bible is everybody healed of his disease. Paul is the greatest of Christian teachers. He wrote more books of the New Testament than any other man. Paul had caught so much of his Master's spirit that he could say (Gal. 2.20): "It is no longer I who live, but Christ who lives in me." An old commentator said that if we had come and knocked at Paul's door and he had responded and we had asked "who lives here?" his answer would have been: "Not Saul of Tarsus, but Jesus of Nazareth." What he was had ceased to be, and what he had become had a better right to Christ's name than his own.

Yet Paul had a bodily affliction that could not be cured: "a thorn was given me in the flesh," he says (2 Cor. 12.7), "a messenger of Satan, to harass me."

Whatever the thorn in the flesh was, he wished it taken away. It seemed such a limiting thing! Without it he could have gone on more journeys, founded more churches, written more letters. He therefore prayed and prayed and prayed that it might be taken away—but it never was and he carried it to his grave. "Three times," he says (2 Cor. 12.8f), "I besought the Lord about this, that it should leave me; but he said to me, 'my grace is sufficient for you, for my power is made perfect in weakness.'"

So triumphant was Paul's own experience that the belief grew up in the early church that physical objects associated with him might transmit healing power. Acts 19.11f tells us that "God did extraordinary miracles by the hands of Paul, so that handkerchiefs or aprons were carried away from his body to the sick, and diseases left them and the evil spirits came out of them." The Book of Acts was written by Luke, and it is notable that this report is set down by a physician who, in the preface to the first volume of his work (Luke 1.1-4), tells us of the careful historical research he had undertaken. It is not said that Paul encouraged this kind of thing. He did not send "handkerchiefs or aprons . . . from his body to the sick." Luke reports the thing impersonally, and is careful to make it clear that credulous people did this on their own: "handkerchiefs or aprons were carried."

It is understandable that beneficial results could flow from this procedure. Objects associated with those we love and admire have always a calming, healing power, as do also souvenirs of significant events in which we have participated. A flower pressed between the pages of a book reminds us of a couple of the days when love was young. Time was when women, who now play bridge, spent their afternoons in handwork: tatting, knitting, crocheting, quilting. A handmade table cloth or quilt or bedspread reminds us of the infinite care and patience mother used to bestow upon the needful business of living. Chocolate pie, made from grandmother's recipe, brings back the wonder of childhood visits to her home. A dog sent to the boarding kennels for a week will be happier if he can take with him a bone he is used to gnawing on. A child who goes away from home for the first time will feel more secure if he can take with him but a single much-loved toy. Amid the strangeness of the unknown, a familiar item may serve to stabilize.

There is nothing magic about such objects. Their value is associational. It is therefore a distortion when people we never heard of advertise that, upon the payment of the proper sum, they will send us a handkerchief which has healing power. Around the world there is great traffic in relics. A drop of the Virgin's milk, the bones of a saint, pieces of the "true" cross—all these are advertised as having wondrous power. Whatever power they possess, however, lies in ourselves rather than in the objects. If they serve to bring before us the heroism of the martyrs, they may help us patiently to endure. Shakespeare tells, concerning Julius Caesar, how a man will

> "beg a hair of him for memory
> And, dying, mention it within his will
> Bequeathing it as a rich legacy
> Unto his issue."

It is in this realm that we are to see the effectiveness of the shaman or medicine man of primitive tribes. His grimaces, dances, and trickery can have no effect upon cancer, bacterial infections, nor upon arteriosclerosis, or other degenerative afflictions. Many of his patients are spared these anyway, since they often die in the prime of life, either of accident or in battle. Witchcraft can effect marvelous cures, however, where the affliction has been induced by mental or social factors. Professor Nathaniel Sherman, of Yale University, discussed the case of a patient upon whom four major operations—all of them unsuccessful—had been performed to cure an affliction which originated outside the body. "A primitive shaman," he said, "might well have cured this case in his first attempt, and even if he had failed four times he would not have endangered the life of the patient on each occasion."

It is clear therefore that articles of clothing associated with Paul could have cured those whose diseases originated in the mind. It is not true, however, that Paul had a panacea. Even when he was personally present he could not cure everybody. The letter to Philippians relates how Epaphroditus had come from Philippi to Rome; "your messenger," Paul calls him (Phil. 2.25), "and minister to my need." Perhaps as a result of the rigors of the journey or of diseases contracted en route, Epaphroditus became very sick. "Indeed he was ill," says Paul (Phil. 2.27, 30), "near to death . . . he nearly died for the work of Christ." Why did not Paul spare him this affliction and misery? Evidently he could not. He does give thanks for ultimate recovery: "God had mercy on him, and not only on him but on me also, lest I should have sorrow upon sorrow" (Phil. 2.27).

Man is mortal. He lives in a house of clay which is subject to swift dissolution. He abides in a tent which may soon have to be taken down. This is an elemental fact about the

body which all must accept. This, however, is not the Bible's
final word on this point. "For we know," says Paul (2 Cor.
5.1), "that if this earthly tent we live in is destroyed, we have
a building from God, a house not made with hands, eternal
in the heavens." One of our Lord's parables suggests that,
even in that realm, however, we shall not settle down. The
story of the dishonest steward concludes with the words:
"make friends for yourselves by means of unrighteous mam-
mon, so that when it fails they may receive you into the
eternal habitations" (Luke 16.9). The phrase translated "the
eternal habitations" is, in the Greek, "eternal tents"—as if in
God's nearer presence we should still be pilgrims of the way.
Meanwhile, we must make the best of the life that now is.

5. *Pure Food*

It was not until modern chemistry and miscroscopy made
possible the analyzing of food substances that nations in the
western world got around to legislation safeguarding the
food supply. Britain enacted its first food law in 1860, the
United States in 1906. The latter resulted from the efforts of
Dr. Harvey W. Wiley, an Indiana chemist who wrote a book
on *Foods and Their Adulteration*. The early law, amended
in 1912, 1913, and 1919, was replaced in 1938 by a stricter
Food, Drug, and Cosmetic Act, now administered by the
Food and Drug Administration of the Federal Security
Agency. National laws regulating food transported from one
state to another are supplemented by local enactments re-
quiring those who handle food to be licensed, in order that
the spread of disease may be prevented.

One provision of our national law forbids the sale of any product that comes from a diseased animal or one that died in any way but slaughter. Leviticus (7.24) contains a similar regulation: "The fat of an animal that dies of itself, and the fat of one that is torn by beasts, may be put to any other use, but on no account shall you eat it."

The Old Testament sacrificial system provides that certain animals are to be offered as evidence of the worshiper's desire to be set right with God. The wondrous process of childbirth has always left the parents with a sense of awe. To find oneself a cocreator with God fills men and women with a sense of unworthiness. The Hebrew law is aware of this elemental feeling and provides that, after childbirth, the mother "shall bring to the priest at the door of the tent of meeting a lamb a year old for a burnt offering" (Lev. 12.6). Provision is made for those not able to provide so costly a gift: "If she cannot afford a lamb, then she shall take two turtledoves or two young pigeons" (Lev. 12.8). It is an interesting commentary upon the home in Nazareth that Joseph and Mary went up to Jerusalem "to offer a sacrifice according to what is said in the law of the Lord, 'a pair of turtledoves or two young pigeons'" (Luke 2.24).

Primitive ideas of sacrifice were that the ascending smoke of a burnt offering provided "a pleasing odor to the LORD" (Lev. 1.9, 13; 3.5, etc.).

The worshiper ate part of the animal, and part was offered in sacrifice; thus God and man were sharers in a common meal. The New Testament declares that "it is impossible that the blood of bulls and goats should take away sins" (Heb. 10.4). The system of animal sacrifice is no longer valid. But lest our enlightened age sneer too much at the ancients, one provision of the law regarding sacrifice ought to be noted. When an animal is presented, the priest "shall offer its fat, the fat tail entire, taking it away close by the backbone, and the fat that covers the entrails, and all the fat that is on the entrails, and the two kidneys with the fat that is on them ... And the priest shall burn it on the altar as food offered by fire to the LORD" (Lev. 3.9-11). This was a kind of Jack Sprat arrangement which prevented the people from eating the fat (Lev. 3.17). In view of doctors' warnings against excessive fat in the diet of twentieth century Americans, it is impressive that the Scripture gives a religious sanction to limitation of fat intake.

In order to govern the food supply, our nation has a Department of Agriculture, which makes regulations regarding the storing of surplus, reduction of acreage to prevent a surplus, proper methods of farming in order to promote soil conservation. The Levitical law also had a code for agriculture. When a fruit tree was planted: "three years it shall be forbidden to you, it must not be eaten. And in the fourth year all their fruit shall be holy, an offering of praise to the LORD. But in the fifth year you may eat of their fruit, that they may yield more richly for you" (Lev. 19.23-25). Our scientists, knowing about rotation of crops, know that land, in order to be most productive, must occasionally be fallow. Leviticus (25.3f) says: "Six years you shall sow your field, and six years you shall prune your vineyard and gather in its fruits; but in the seventh year there shall be a sabbath of solemn rests for the land."

Conservation of natural resources for the public good is enjoined also (Deut. 20.19f). Moses is represented as instructing his people that when they go into the land they are to possess and capture its cities, "you shall not destroy its trees by wielding an axe against them; for you may eat of them, but you shall not cut them down ... Only the trees which you know are not trees for food you may destroy and cut down that you may build siegeworks." It is notable, too, that some natural resources were to be kept intact for the benefit of the community: "The fields of common land belonging to their cities may not be sold" (Lev. 25.34).

The reasons for prejudices for and against certain forms of food are difficult to fathom. The French regularly eat horse meat, and shops which sell it are as numerous as "butcher" shops which deal in the flesh of other animals. The reason why those of British descent do not eat horse meat is said to be bound up with the conversion of the Saxons to Christianity. In their pagan state the Saxons worshiped, among other deities, Woden, whose name survives in our Wednesday. Woden—called Odin by the Norse and Wotan by Wagner—was the god of battle and protector of dead heroes. Perhaps for this reason the horse, powerful in battle, was sacred to him. When the Saxons became Christians, therefore, horse flesh was forbidden to them as a symbol of their separation from the old life and its ways.

Among many ancient peoples, pigs, with their large litters, were regarded as a fine example of the productive power of nature, and hence a worthy sacrifice to the deities who presided over fertility. At the festival of the full moon, the Egyptians offered pigs in honor of Isis and Osiris. The Athenians, the Romans and the Boeotians all are said to have offered swine in their mystery cults. Isaiah (65.4) speaks of some

> "who sit in tombs,
> and spend the night in secret places;
> who eat swine's flesh,
> and broth of abominable things is in their vessels."

Isaiah (66.3 and 17) included other references to those who offer "swine's blood" and eat "swine's flesh."

Perhaps it was because of this identification with pagan rites that the Hebrews shunned the use of pork. Swine became the symbol of defilement and the badge of insult. Proverbs (11.22) says:

"Like a gold ring in a swine's snout
is a beautiful woman without discretion."

Hebrew revulsion against this animal exceeded that toward
any other unclean thing. The scribes declared that "ten
measures of pestilential diseases were spread over the earth,
and nine of them fell to the share of the pigs." So intense was
the feeling against pigs that even the brutish name was
dropped and the pious substituted for it the phrase, "the
other thing."

This attitude is important for our understanding of two
passages in the Gospels. It was in "a far country" that the
prodigal "joined himself to one of the citizens of that country,
who sent him into the fields to feed swine" (Luke 15.15).
That could not have happened in the homeland! Moreover,
our Lord no doubt chose this detail to suggest the most ig-
nominious depth to which a Hebrew could sink—nursemaid
to pigs!

The swine mentioned in Matthew (8.30) were probably
maintained by Gentiles for soldiers of the Roman legion. Explaining that demons left a possessed man and entered into
the swine, Matthew (8.32) relates that "the whole herd
rushed down the steep bank into the sea and perished in the
waters." Is this Matthew's way of telling us that the wild
man's gestures frightened the creatures into stampeding? Or
does it reflect the Hebrew point of view that such a cata-
strophic loss would serve anybody right who kept animals of
that sort?

Americans are not fond of locusts—but Near Easterners regard their edibility as atonement for the crop devastation
their presence brings. Various recipes seem to have been in
use to make them appetizing. They could be broiled or
stewed or fried in butter. They could be mixed with butter
and spread on thin layers of bread—oriental version of the

canape. More generally, they are thrown alive into a rapidly boiling pot of salted water. Taken out after a few minutes, the heads, wings, and feet are thrown away, and their bodies are dried in the oven or on the roof-top. They may then be ground and baked into cakes or else put away in bags for winter use. There are shops in some eastern cities which deal in locusts strung on cords as vendors in the western world dispense peanuts or candy. Matthew (3.4) tells us of John the Baptizer; "his food was locusts and wild honey." The prophet may have been eccentric, but his diet is no evidence of it.

The Biblical description of these creatures is not anatomically accurate. Leviticus (11.21) declares that "among the winged insects that go on all fours you may eat those which have legs above their feet." By definition, an insect has at least three pairs of legs, and does not "go on all fours." Having "legs above their feet" seems to be a way of saying that the hindmost pair of legs is longer and stronger than that of ordinary insects. The King James Version at this point is even more curious: "which have knees above their hinder legs." The Levitical permission to eat locusts includes the related species: "the bald locust according to its kind, the cricket according to its kind, and the grasshopper according to its kind. But all other winged insects which have four feet are an abomination to you" (Lev. 11.22f).

Rabbinical regulation provided criteria for identifying the kinds of locusts that were permitted for food. They must have four front feet and two springing feet, four wings so long and broad as to cover the greater portion of the body. Creatures with these characteristics were considered edible, without reference to the shape of the head, whether round or oblong, and without reference to the presence or absence of a tail.

With all these dietary regulations, there was much ado in

our Lord's time about clean and unclean foods. These questions still are debated. Vegetarians—among whom the distinguished playwright, Bernard Shaw was vociferously numbered—consider that a sensible human diet will exclude meat, fish, and fowl. Vegetarians are not united. Some exclude not only animals but all animal products, and this includes butter and eggs; for cow's milk they substitute coconut milk. Some permit the use of fish caught in a net, but not fish caught on a hook.

Hindu vegetarianism, coupled with veneration of the cow, has led to an overpopulation of cows in India, with a consequent decline in food for little children. Vegetarianism is a principle of the Seventh Day Adventists. Every four years, the Vegetarian Party nominates a man to run for president of the United States. There are popular notions that certain foods are good for certain parts of the body. Fish, for example, is said to be good brain food. Doctors hold that this is as absurd as to say that jello is good food for the big toe.

Jesus did not suggest the abandonment of discrimination with regard to what seemed edible. He did make it clear that God's favor does not depend upon what kind of food we eat! To Pharisees greatly concerned with dietary laws Jesus said: "Hear and understand: not what goes into the mouth defiles a man, but what comes out of the mouth, this defiles a man" (Mt. 15.10, 11). When this revolutionary statement was met with protest, he went on: "Do you not see that whatever goes into the mouth passes into the stomach and so passes on? But what comes out of the mouth proceeds from the heart, and this defiles a man. For out of the heart come evil thoughts, murder, adultery, fornication, theft, false witness, slander. These are what defile a man" (Mt. 15.17-20). Life on this basis is not the way to a ripe old age. The Scripture points to another way.

6. The Evergreen Life

Scientists who, by examining tree rings, study the age of forests, tell us that the oldest living things on our planet are pine trees growing in the upper timber line of mountains in eastern California. Genesis (5.27) relates that Methuselah lived to the ripe old age of 969, but these trees have already lived four times as long as he. Bristlecone pines in the White Mountains, twenty miles northeast of Bishop, Calif., are believed to be something like 4100 years of age, making them 900 years older than the oldest giant sequoia, thought to have been alive for 3200 years. The oldest pine tree was about to celebrate its first millennium when the oldest sequoia was but a seedling.

The great age of the bristlecone pines is accompanied by slow growth. Their stem thickness is 25 to 50 inches, their height 15 to 30 feet. The quantity of wood found in the largest sequoia would be a thousand times as great as the volume in a bristlecone pine. But the pine is sturdy enough to survive flood and drought and the climatic changes of forty centuries. The California pine trees were living when Abraham set out from Ur of the Chaldees, not knowing where he was to go!

It is significant that the oldest of living things has been found to be an evergreen. The first Psalm tells us that the good man leads an evergreen life:

> "He is like a tree
>   planted by streams of water,
>   that yields its fruit in its season
>   and its leaf does not wither."

The newly discovered Dead Sea Scrolls,[1] which reflect ancient Jewish piety, frequently use this imagery:

"I am as a tree
  green beside streams of water,
  bearing fruit, abounding in leaves."

The *Manual of Discipline* is sure that as long as Israel has a company of men well versed in the Law, "the community will rest securely on a basis of truth. It will become a plant evergreen." God has chosen His faithful ones to form

"a fabric of holiness,
  a plant evergreen,
    for all time to come."

The men who are in communion with God

"shall yield a flower unfading,
  the twig shall put forth thick leaves,
    become an evergreen."

"Thy Law, O God, is an evergreen," sings another of the Qumran Psalms. Good men live where there

"stand planted for Thy glory alone,
  the trees that never die,
  the fir, the pine, and the cypress,

            . . . . . .

  putting forth branches unfading."

In Psalm 52 the life of the wicked is contrasted with that of the upright. The latter will laugh at the former, saying:

"'See the man who would not make God his refuge,
  but trusted in the abundance of his riches,
  and sought refuge in his wealth'

[1] Quotations of the Dead Sea Scrolls are from *The Dead Sea Scriptures*, by Theodor H. Gaster. Copyright 1956 by Theodor H. Gaster, reprinted by permission of Doubleday and Co., Inc.

'But I am like a green olive tree
 in the house of God
I trust in the steadfast love of God
 for ever and ever' " (Psalm 52.7f).

Olive trees, too, attain a great age, and their fruitfulness
makes them a symbol of those who put their trust in the
Eternal.

Psalm 92.12f tells us that the people of God

"grow like a cedar in Lebanon,
They are planted in the house of the LORD,
 they flourish in the courts of our God.
They still bring forth fruit in old age,
 they are full of sap and green."

The REVISED STANDARD VERSION at this point is in striking
contrast with the King James Version, which reads: "Those
that be planted in the house of the Lord shall flourish in the
courts of our God. They shall still bring forth fruit in old
age: they shall be fat and flourishing." Which is the true
picture of the mature condition of the wise man, "fat and
flourishing" or "full of sap and green"? Correct translation
here accords with observations arising from human experience. The next verse goes on to point out that the condition
of the good man in old age vindicates the justice of God.
Both translations render the next words: "to show that the
LORD is upright."

A man who has dedicated his life to the care of the aged
confesses that the REVISED STANDARD VERSION brought him
great relief. In presenting his cause to the churches, he is accustomed to speak from the text, "They still bring forth fruit
in old age." "Ofttimes it has wounded me," he writes, "to
note that the second part of that text in the King James Version is just exactly opposite to one of my main points, which
is that people should not eat enough to become fat, and that

if they do become fat they will not flourish but will probably
pass out much sooner, each few pounds of weight taking off
one year at the end of life. The putting on of excess weight
hastens the aging process, reduces the sap, and makes life
wither rather than remain green. The King James," he continues "also has this fattening process to be for the purpose
of showing that God is upright, whereas it shows just the
opposite."

If the Bible encourages people to eat until they become
fat, he believes this would be a denial of the standard of uprightness by which God runs His world. The Bible makes ap-
proving reference to fat cattle, but cattle are among the most
unresponsive of animals—they are a kind of machine for turning grass into milk. The REVISED STANDARD VERSION clarifies
other Biblical references to fatness. At Isaiah (58.11) the
King James says: "The Lord shall guide thee continually,
and make fat thy bones." The REVISED STANDARD VERSION
here reads:

> "And the Lord will guide you continually,
>   and satisfy your desire with good things,
>   and make your bones strong" (compare Prov. 15.30).

On the other hand, fatness is used by the prophet Isaiah
to describe the condition of indifference, which deadens the
senses of those who hear God's word without responding:

> "Make the heart of this people fat,
>   and their ears heavy" (Is. 6.10;

compare the use of this passage in Matthew 13.14f to describe the strange reason for parables).

Death by automobile is said now to lead the mortality rate
among a certain group of young people. Traffic accidents
have multiplied at such a frightening rate that the churches
and synagogues of a Connecticut community conducted a

campaign to reduce slaughter on the highway. The ministers and rabbis of Greenwich all preached from the text, "You shall not kill" (Ex. 20.13), making a twentieth-century application of the age-old commandment. This item from the Decalogue is ordinarily interpreted as a prohibition of murder, but the Connecticut divines found it an appropriate injunction for speeders.

By some of the Reformers this commandment was interpreted also as a prohibition against overeating. One of the seventeenth-century catechisms asks: "What are the duties required in the sixth commandment?" and answers: "The duties required in the sixth commandment are all careful studies, and lawful endeavors to preserve the life of ourselves and others, resisting all thoughts and purposes, and avoiding all occasions, temptations, and practices, which tend to the unjust taking away of the life of any ... a sober use of meat, drink, physic, sleep, labor, and recreation." Sleeping too much, playing too much and eating too much are here interpreted as violations of the command, "You shall not kill."

The man who eats too much, in a sense, commits suicide, since, by hastening the day of his death, he deprives himself of a part of life. Doctors tell us that overeating may manifest itself in foot trouble, kidney disease, and some types of cancer. Dr. Paul Dudley White, President Eisenhower's consultant, said that overeating "may play even more of a role in the destiny of the world than malnutrition." Excess intake of food, he told the European Congress of Cardiology, might lead directly to high blood pressure and this to heart trouble, and so become "a factor in the universal threat of coronary heart disease in the leading citizens of the world."

One doctor says that the only advantage fat gives is ability to float, and that "our overweight citizens are our greatest nutritional failures." This is a problem not only in well-fed

America but in other parts of the world, too. The British Association for the Advancement of Science reports that waistlines in Britain are "growing alarmingly." A dispatch from Munich says that "Overeating is becoming to West Germany almost as great a curse as alcoholism is to France." The unforeseen effects of this gluttony are as startling as they are far-reaching. Automobile cushions and theatre chairs are now too narrow. Railway seats designed to accommodate four passengers will take only three. The textile industry has had to expand from 148 to 160 centimeters the width of cloth for men's suits.

It is hardly necessary to add that the medical profession reports an upsurge in diabetes and circulatory ailments. Hebrews (12.1) says: "Let us also lay aside every weight . . . and . . . run with perseverance the race that is set before us." This is a picturesque way of describing the Christian life, but may also apply to the body which is the temple of the spirit.

He who would run a race plans not even to carry the needless weight of excess clothing. No one setting out for a walk suspends a 25-pound bag of sugar from his shoulders, but some do try to go through life with burdens even greater. These are bound to have their effect upon the human frame, even as a machine would be thrown out of balance and worn unevenly if a sack of flour were strapped to a flywheel. For a human being to carry around too much excess weight is to wear himself out, keep himself too lethargic for spiritual vigor, and shorten life. The good man is not like a cow, "fat and flourishing," but like a tree that is "ever full of sap and green." Such blessedness does not just happen; it is the result of self-discipline. The Scripture speaks, too, of that.

7. Temperance or Self-Control?

Fat men do not make good soldiers. The extra weight they carry around makes it difficult for them to sustain the long marches and endure the hardships when the going becomes tough. A commanding officer in the United States Army decided that his troops were too fat. For the benefit of the overweight, he posted in the mess halls a sign with the heading, "Operation Bulge," and the slogan, "You cannot lie to the scale." The poster advised the men each day to consume a pint and a half of milk; some lettuce or tomatoes and some citrus fruit; to eat plenty of meat, fish and eggs; not to eat bread, butter, cake, candy, cereals, chocolate, crackers, cream, custard, gravy, icecream, jellies, noodles, nuts, oil, pastry, potatoes, pudding, rice, soups, spaghetti, sugar.

The general was himself a tall, spare man who had had to guzzle malted milks and stuff himself with bananas in order to put on enough weight to pass the physical examination for West Point. He had difficulty understanding how his men could allow themselves to become obese. One regiment estimated that its 3,500 men lost a ton when the reducing order went into effect. Determined to thin his ranks, the general fined some of his men who did not co-operate, and stripped others of their rank.

The army can court-martial a man who will not reduce. The military life generally takes over many functions which a free individual should perform for himself. Obesity is linked with a high rate of disability from degenerative cardiovascular disease, diabetes, and other afflictions; it aggravates and complicates other conditions of the body; it is accompanied by a shortened life expectancy. For those not under military discipline (where others make decisions for them) the Biblical teaching in regard to self-control seems of the first importance.

Older versions of the Scripture relate that Paul before Felix "reasoned of righteousness, temperance, and judgment to come" (Acts 24.25). The REVISED STANDARD VERSION tells us that "he argued about justice and self-control and future judgment." Note that "self-control" is a more inclusive term than "temperance." The basic meaning of the word "temperance" is: "Habitual moderation in the indulgence of the appetites and passions." Among certain groups the term has been given a specialized meaning; it signifies total abstinence from intoxicating beverages. The word, however, properly suggests moderation in food as well as in drink. A "temperance hotel" is one in which no liquor is sold. It does not mean one in which overeating is forbidden.

A Reformation catechism, in enumerating the positive duties required of the sixth commandment, lists: "a sober use of meat, drink, physic, sleep, labor, and recreation." Members of a "temperance" organization held a luncheon at which the table fairly groaned under good and fattening foods which some of the ladies could ill afford to enjoy. After all had partaken bountifully, the hostess said to a visitor: "We don't drink—but we sure do eat!" There is, of course, a difference. When one eats too much, he does not go home to abuse his children and beat up his wife, nor does he drive his car down the wrong side of the road. The Scripture, however, enjoins self-control with respect to food as well as drink.

Wise men among the Hebrews warned against the excessive use of strong drink:

> "Wine is a mocker, strong drink a brawler;
> and whoever is led astray by it is not wise."
> (Prov. 20.1).

"Who has woe? Who has sorrow?
Who has strife? Who has complaining?
Who has wounds without cause?
Who has redness of eyes?
Those who tarry long over wine,
those who go to try mixed wine.
Do not look at wine when it is red,
when it sparkles in the cup
and goes down smoothly.
At the last it bites like a serpent,
and stings like an adder."
(Prov. 23.29-32).

The Hebrews, however, linked excessive use of food with excessive use of drink:

"Be not among winebibbers,
or among gluttonous eaters of meat;
for the drunkard and the glutton will come to poverty,
and drowsiness will clothe a man with rags"
(Prov. 23.20-21).

The stupor that results from intoxication we call a hangover. Gluttony, too, can lead to a sluggish indolence and drowsy inclination to sleep. One of the Hebrew proverbs has to do with excessive use of sweets:

"If you have found honey, eat only enough for you,
lest you be sated with it and vomit it."
(Proverbs 25.16)

Self-control is the athlete's discipline. This, too, the Bible knows: "Every athlete exercises self-control in all things" (1 Cor. 9.25). What is good for athletes is good also for people in general. Timothy 1 and 2 and Titus are referred to as the Pastoral Epistles because they give us our best picture of organization in the early church. They tell us what administrative offices there were, and what the requirements for these offices were. It was expected of a bishop, for ex-

ample, that he be "self-controlled" (Titus 1.8). This is the
kind of discipline by which a man becomes free to be his
most effective self. It is not the kind of abstinence from food
by which primitive men thought God could be compelled
to do what they wished. Among Mohammedans, fasting is
considered one of the good works by which Allah's favor can
be won.

The Bible denounces this kind of fasting. Jeremiah (14.12)
and Zechariah (7.5) indicate how the God of Israel cannot
be won over by fasting. The prophet Isaiah hears God say:

"Is not this the fast that I choose:
    to loose the bonds of wickedness,
    to undo the thongs of the yoke,
to let the oppressed go free,
    and to break every yoke?
Is it not to share your bread with the hungry,
    and bring the homeless poor into your house;
when you see the naked, to cover him,
    and not to hide yourself from your own flesh?
                                            (Is. 58.6, 7).

Paul is sure that man cannot ever do enough good works
to earn God's favor, as it is by grace that "we have been saved
through faith." Even this is not our "own doing, it is the gift
of God" (Eph. 2.8). The power to receive this gift is itself
a gift. That man cannot buy his salvation does not mean that
he will be indifferent to good works. On the contrary, Paul
is sure that believers are "created in Christ Jesus for good
works, which God compared beforehand, that we should
walk in them" (Eph. 2.10).

For these good works, Paul has another descriptive term.
He calls them the fruit of the Spirit. Although there are so
many of them, he uses the singular term "fruit" in order to
denote their essential unity. This latter is in contrast with
the manifold and diverse "works of the flesh." Evil flourishes
like weeds; good is as a vine. Among these Christian habits

of mind which Paul describes as "the fruit of the Spirit," he lists "self-control" (Gal. 5.23). This is in contrast with the rank growth of wickedness which manifests itself in "drunkenness, carousing, and the like" (Gal. 5.21).

The place of self-control in relation to other qualities is suggested by a kind of chain-of-command outlined in 2 Peter (1.5-7): "make every effort to supplement your faith with virtue, and virtue with knowledge, and knowledge with self-control, and self-control with steadfastness, and steadfastness with godliness, and godliness with brotherly affection, and brotherly affection with love."

It is easier by self-control to avoid the addition of excess poundage than by dieting to remove it. Americans surrounded by Nature's bounty find it easy to eat too much. Reducing diets, therefore, are sought after, and these sometimes promise swift and drastic weight reduction. Doctors warn of the danger in these. Sudden and indiscriminate omission from daily intake of certain elements may result in malnutrition. Some fad diets are below the minimum standard for the maintenance of bodily structure and function.

Where weight needs to be shed, the reduction ought to be carried out under the direction of a physician; judgment as to the proper balance ought not to be left to the uninformed. Far better to abstain in the first place from the delicacies that fatten. A woman complained that her husband, refusing to eat salads and vegetables, termed them "rabbit food." "Tell him," said the doctor, "that middle-aged rabbits don't have a paunch, do have their own teeth, and haven't lost their romantic appeal."

Excess weight can have its effect upon romance. A man whose wife now weighs 120 pounds is fond of relating that when they were married she weighed only 90 pounds. "In the marriage ceremony," he says, "I promised to love and to cherish the woman she then was. But she has become something other than that, and there is now 25 per cent of her for which I have no responsibility." He really adores her, and says this only to tease. Women who weigh 90 pounds can usually afford to increase their weight by 30 pounds, but a bride of 120 pounds who increased her weight in the same proportion would tip the scales at 160—and her husband might really find it harder to be romantic about one who had grown so much larger than she whom he pledged himself to "comfort, honor, and keep in sickness and in health."

Husbands may not be blameless when their wives take on too much weight. When people are starved for affection, they sometimes try to make up for it by stuffing themselves with great quantities of food. In this realm, as in all others, there is a mutuality between husband and wife which means that one is not blameless in the other's failure. Temperance is a good thing, but the Bible enjoins a better. To rule one's own self is better than to capture a city, and "the fruit of the spirit is self-control." Even when we fail, God still sends the messengers of His love. To some of these, the name which the Bible gives is "angels."

8. Angel of Healing

At a time when God was thought to be far away, it was believed that He required assistants in order to keep in touch with His Creation. There developed therefore a belief in intermediaries called angels—the term means messenger. Many acts of creation and providence, originally attributed to God Himself, in later Judaism were ascribed to angels. Genesis (2.19) relates that when God had created "every beast of the field and every bird of the air" he brought them to Adam "to see what he would call them." In the Book of

Jubilees, however, God is too aloof for this contact with His creatures, and it is angels who bring the animals to Adam. Genesis (6.14ff) represents God as telling Noah how the ark is to be constructed. Enoch (1) ascribes the building of the ark to angels. In Exodus (20) God gives the Law to Moses. Galatians (3.19), however, tells us that the law "was ordained by angels through an intermediary."

Revelation (8.2) speaks of "the seven angels who stand before God." These are no doubt the seven archangels familiar in Jewish thought. The number may have been derived from foreign sources. Gathered here as courtiers about the heavenly king, they resemble the seven counselors at the Persian court mentioned in Ezra (7.14). Zoroastrianism had a hierarchy of celestial beings. In the earliest portions of the Bible, there is no indication that some angels had higher rank than others, and the thought of a specially privileged group may have been derived from Iranian sources. In any case, three of the seven archangels are mentioned by name in the Scripture. One reveals God's will to man; one is concerned with man's safety; one has responsibility in the realm of healing.

Within both Testaments the angel Gabriel appears as the messenger of God. He is the bearer of revelation to Daniel (Daniel 8.15f; 9.21f), and in Luke (1.26; compare 1.11f) the story of the Annunciation tells how "in the sixth month the angel Gabriel was sent from God to a city of Galilee." Jewish commentators identified Gabriel as the angel who had performed other specific functions. He was the man who found Joseph "wandering in the fields" (Gen. 37.15) and gave him directions. He officiated at the burial of Moses (Deut. 34.6), and he was the one who destroyed the army of Sennacherib (2 Chron. 32.21).

In Jesus' conflict with those determined to put him out of the way, our Lord renounced the "more than twelve legions of angels" (Mt. 26.53) who might have been summoned to his side. Mohammed, however, claimed that in opposing the idolatrous Meccans he had 3,000 angels fighting for him, with Gabriel at their head. Mohammed held also that Gabriel was the revealer of the Koran. Swedenborgians hold that there is in heaven a society of angels called Gabriel. It is composed of thousands of angels, but "societies of angels, when seen from a great distance, appear as stars," and the society called Gabriel was the star the Wise Men saw (Mt. 2.1f). In 1951, Pope Pius XII appointed Gabriel as the patron saint of the radio and television industry.

Michael, another of the archangels, appears in the Scripture as the patron and champion of Israel. His name means "Who is like unto God." In Daniel 10.21 he is described as the nation's "prince" and in Daniel 12.1 as the deliverer of his people in the time of trouble. In some of the inter-testamental literature he is pictured as instructing Moses on Sinai and delivering to him the tables of the law; as the recording angel who enters the deeds of all men on the heavenly books; as interceding for the just, and mediating peace to Israel. Jude (9) tells how "the archangel Michael, contending with the devil, disputed about the body of Moses." Finally in Revelation (12.7-9) "Michael and his angels" fight against the dragon. Here it is the archangel Michael, rather than the Messiah, who is the leader of the people as they overthrow the archenemy of God.

Raphael was the angel who presided over healing. His name indeed means "God has healed."

Rabbinical literature speaks of a Book of Noah, which was one of the earliest treatises on medicine. The tradition is that after the flood men were afflicted with various diseases, and God sent the angel Raphael to reveal to Noah the curative property of plants and roots.

Both in the Old Testament and in the New, the birth of

Isaac to Sarah in her old age is thought of as a glorious illustration of how God, in order to keep His promise, would do unexpected things. That "Sarah herself received power to conceive even when she was past the age" is listed in Hebrews 11.11 as one of the mighty acts of faith and in Romans (4.19) Paul says that "Abraham did not weaken in faith" even though he "was as good as dead because he was about a hundred years old, or when he considered the barrenness of Sarah's womb." Ancient Jewish interpreters held that Raphael was one of the three visitors who appeared to Abraham in Genesis (18), and that the purpose of Raphael's coming was to make it possible for Sarah to have a child.

In the book of Tobit, when Tobias sets out on a long and difficult journey, his father is uneasy about him until the angel Raphael promises, "I will go with you, for I know the way." Disguised as a guide or dragoman, Raphael does accompany Tobias on the entire route. The guardian angel still is real to multitudes in Christendom. In the "Completion Litany" of the Greek Orthodox Church there is this petition: "For an angel of peace, a faithful guide, a guardian of our souls and bodies, let us beseech the Lord." In Sabine Baring-Gould's much-loved evening hymn, beginning "Now the day is over," the fourth stanza reads:

> "Through the long night watches,
> May Thine angels spread
> Their white wings above me,
> Watching round my bed."

Raphael not only accompanies Tobias on his journey but he also performs two specific acts of healing. Tobit has been blinded by bird-dung that had fallen into his eyes, but Tobit is a just man. He has not neglected to give alms or to bury the dead, and so Raphael restores his sight. Sarah, whom Tobias hoped to marry, had already had seven husbands, each of whom had been stricken dead upon entering the marriage chamber. Asmodeus, the demon, was in love with her and therefore attacked any who dared approach her. Raphael provided Tobias with a medical potion, "the heart and liver of a fish" which had power to exorcise the demon. Being thus thwarted, Asmodeus, "fled to remotest parts of Egypt."

Since God became incarnate, man has not felt the need of such intermediaries. On the higher levels of New Testament thought, angels are associated with the old world order which, since Christ came, is on its way out. In Romans (8.39) angels apparently are thought of as hostile to man's salvation; not even they "will be able to separate us from the love of God." Paul therefore in the letter to Colossians deplores the adoration which some there were offering these celestial beings: "Let no one disqualify you," he says (2.18), "insisting on self-abasement and worship of angels."

Two New Testament letters make it clear that God in Christ has done for His Church far greater things than He ever did for angels. Ephesians (3.10) speaks of God's purpose "that through the church the manifold wisdom of God might now be made known to the principalities and powers in the heavenly places." I Peter (1.12) speaks of the good news which has been preached to the church as containing "things into which angels long to look." The Greek here pictures them standing, as it were, on tiptoe, straining to get a better view of that which so excites their attention. At best, then, angels seem only to have a contemplative share in the work of redemption. As Charles Wesley sings:

> "Angels in fix'd amazement
> Around our altars hover,
> With eager gaze
> Adore the grace
> Of our Eternal Lover."

We may therefore believe that with respect to healing God has done a greater thing for us than He did for the ancients. The true significance of angels will lie in what they symbolize. Jesus did not deem it necessary to clarify popular notions on the subject, since those who believed in them certainly believed in a God whose loving activity had ways of making itself felt in the life of man. One aspect of this surely is the care of the sick and helpless. From earliest times this has been undertaken by both men and women, although most fully developed under Christianity. Raphael, representing God's healing work, did not despise the use of means. While masculine terms are used of angels, they are most often thought of in our time as feminine.

A hundred years ago, Florence Nightingale began to put nursing on a professional basis. In 1854 she organized a hospital unit for the Crimean War. At Scutari and Balaklava she "enforced discipline, introduced sanitary reforms and, against opposition, secured necessary supplies." In 1860, with the testimonial fund given her for her war services, she established in London the "Nightingale School and Home for training nurses." For her work among suffering soldiers she was called "the angel of Balaklava."

So many a patient can say, with George Pope Morris:

> " 'Tis ever thus, when in life's storm
> Hope's star to man grows dim.
> An angel kneels, in woman's form,
> And breathes a prayer for him."

The Scripture, too, sets forth the tenderness of those who in this fashion serve the Divine purpose. Paul actually uses a feminine term to describe his relationship with the dearly loved residents of Macedonia. "We were gentle among you," he says (I Thess. 2.7), "like a nurse taking care of her children." The picture in the Greek is of a mother suckling her child and keeping it warm at her bosom. If any one thinks of Paul as a stern, if reformed, Pharisee, dealing in theological abstractions, let him ponder that figure of speech and the mind that could think it up!

The Old Testament mentions nursing fathers (Num. 11.12; Is. 49.23). In wealthy families of the Near East a poor relation is sometimes appointed to this office. It is his duty to be the playmate, the guardian, and the constant companion of the heir. He must carry him when he is tired, and his is the responsibility of giving the lad his first lessons in horsemanship and manly sports. Thomas Fuller refers to "Princes, who should be nursing fathers and suckle the church." The New Testament, however, is true to the divinely established order. Paul does not describe himself as a nursing father but as a nursing mother. To angels is assigned still another function in the Scripture. To that we turn.

9. Angel of Water

It is said of one ecclesiastic that he knew all the angels' birthdays and what color socks they wore. Of all that there is nothing in the Gospels. Jesus' infrequent references to angels reflect the common views in Palestine, and give no evidence that he regarded them as needful for the soul's communication with its Maker. Some consider it entirely natural that among the orders of creation there should be individuals who owe their existence not to parents, but to the immediate creative will of God. On the other hand, there are those who consider that twentieth century man must "reject, or ignore as superfluous, the ministry of angels." It seems rather that we should see in them a religious view of the world, which everywhere recognizes the power of God going forth to accomplish His will.

Sholem Asch, trained in Hebrew lore, pictures the part which familiar ideas played in the education of Jesus. In Asch's book *Mary*, angels have frequent commerce with humans. With "unseen sign and invisible finger," one of them summoned Mary, and she "felt the noiseless shadow of two mighty wings quivering above her head." Joseph, though he saw no wings, "felt upon his cheek the cooling breath of air stirred by their flutter." Explaining all this to her Son, Mary says: "God has many hands, and they are called His angels." The Scripture represents these "hands" as assigned to various functions.

Revelation (14.18) refers to "the angel who has power over fire." This "angel came out from the altar" and is associated, presumably, with the fires of incense burning there. Psalm 104.4 is part of a prayer addressed to God

> "who makest the winds thy messengers,
> fire and flame thy ministers."

Upon the basis of that passage, the rabbis held that angels were of fiery disposition. The former of those two lines was perhaps in the mind of the apocalyptist when he "saw four angels standing at the four corners of the earth holding back the four winds of the earth."

Men's thoughts pass readily from wind to spirit and from spirit to prayer. In Revelation (5.8) and (8.3) angels are represented as carrying men's prayers up to God. The imagery here, however, is highly symbolic and "the prayers of the saints" are pictured as "golden bowls full of incense." When Jacob fell asleep and dreamed at Bethel, "there was a ladder set upon the earth, and the top of it reached to heaven; and behold, the angels of God were ascending and descending on it" (Gen. 28.12). Since they ascended before they descended, it is assumed that their abode was with men. In the Sermon on the Mount, Jesus bids us: "pray to your Father who is in secret; and your father who sees in secret will reward you" (Mt. 6.6). No need here for angels' help in prayer!

In the Shepherd of Hermas, an early Christian writing found in some of the oldest New Testaments, there is an angel of repentance who says: "Go and tell all men to repent, and they shall live unto God." In 2 Kings (21.11-15) we are told how God's anger was great against the wicked King Manasseh. On account of him, said God, "I am bringing upon Jerusalem and Judah such evil that the ears of every one who hears it will tingle." In 2 Chronicles (33.11-13), however, it is related that Manasseh, chastened by punishment and exile, "humbled himself greatly before the God of his fathers. He prayed to him and God received his entreaty." The prayer which Manasseh prayed appears among the canticles appended to the Psalms in some old manuscripts, and appears in many versions of the Apocrypha. Because Manasseh had been so wicked, however, forgiveness for him was a problem for the rabbis. Some held that when he repented, the angels of the Presence blocked up the way by which man's prayers reach the throne of God, whereupon God made a way under His throne which angels could not reach.

In Revelation (16.5) mention is made of "the angel of water." The early church fathers connected this with baptism. Ambrose and Chrysostom saw in this passage a prophecy of the descent of the Holy Spirit consecrating the waters of baptism to the mystical washing away of sin. Tertullian saw in it a reference to the baptismal angel. A sixth century Egyptian monk connected it with the Biblical cosmology. Genesis (7.11) relates, in connection with the flood which came upon the earth in the days of Noah, that " the windows of the heavens were opened." Malachi (3.10) contains a conditional promise that He will "open the windows of heaven." Cosmas Indicopleustes held that angels were assigned to the duty of opening and closing the heavenly windows in order that the earth might be refreshed with an outpouring from "the waters which were above the firmament" (Gen. 1.7).

It was a common belief in the ancient world, however, that angels were associated with water. This is reflected in the Old Testament in the story of Jacob at Jabbok. Having got his family and goods safely across the ford, the patriarch lay down to sleep beside the stream. Genesis (32.24) tells us that "Jacob was left alone; and a man wrestled with him until the breaking of the day." This was probably a reference to the angel whose province it was to preside over that particular body of water. To this day, primitive people will make no effort to rescue a drowning man. If he has fallen into the stream it is because he is in the clutches of the angel of the water, and any effort to snatch him away would be to endanger oneself.

In the New Testament there is the story of a man who, ill for 38 years, hoped to be cured at the pool of Bethzatha, in Jerusalem. When Jesus appeared, the patient asked for help, with the explanation: "Sir, I have no man to put me into the pool when the water is troubled, and while I am going another steps down before me" (John 5.7). The popular belief seems to have been that when the water began to bubble, the first patient to enter received relief, but that all others had to wait some other turn. What made the water bubble? The pool was evidently subject to periodic disturbance as the result of water gushing up from an intermittent spring.

In the mind of the people, however, such an upsurge could be explained only by the activity of an angel. John (5:4) in the King James Version reads: "For an angel went down at a certain season into the pool, and troubled the water: whosoever then first after the troubling of the water stepped in was made whole of whatsoever disease he had." This verse, however, does not appear at all in the REVISED STANDARD VERSION, which jumps from verse 3 to verse 5. This is because the passage is not found in the oldest manuscripts. Not part of the original, it was an addition written into the margin by some scribe who was sure that any curative power in a spring must be attributed to the angel of water. Commenting on this passage, a fourth century preacher said: "An angel came down and troubled the water, and endowed it with healing power, that the Jews might learn that much more could the Lord of angels heal the diseases of the soul."

Modern man does not speak of angels as causing water to bubble up with healing power, but the popularity of such European resorts as Bath (England), Spa (Belgium), Aix-les-Bains (France), Baden-Baden (Germany), and Karls-bad (Czechoslovakia), as well as such American place names as Mineral Wells (Tex.), French Lick (Ind.), White Sulphur Springs (W. Va.), and Hot Springs (Ark.) attest man's continuing conviction that pools of water do have curative value. The water issuing from many springs does contain such mineral salts as "carbonates, chlorides, phosphates, silicates, sulphides and sulphates of calcium, iron, lithium, magnesium, potassium, sodium, and other metals." Present, sometimes, also are such gases as carbon dioxide (which gives sparkle to soda water). Some mineral springs are hot and are therefore called thermal.

Such descriptive terms are hardly as poetic as the ancient conception of an angel who presided over water. Our age thinks it has discovered causes when it only traces sequence! Angel or no, the springs of earth are often recommended as of value in the treatment of "rheumatism, gout, liver trouble, blood ailments, dyspepsia, and many of the common diseases of various organs and parts of the human body."

A scientist wrote a book called *Water: Miracle of Nature* (by Thomson King: Macmillan, 1953). Francis of Assisi sang: "Praised be my Lord for our sister water." He thought of us all as children of "our mother the earth," and water as our sister. In England and Scotland a nurse is not called a nurse but a sister. Water is that kind of sister. Its use in medicine is called hydrotherapy. A physician writes that knowledge of "water treatment would be a safer and really better thing for the home doctors and nurses than the knowledge of drugs which most of them profess." Preissnitz bandage is the name given to a cloth wrung out of cool water and placed on the abdomen. There are some forms of abdominal pain in which this is said by doctors to be as effective as morphine. A hot compress on the nose and a cold compress on the throat are sometimes recommended in treatment of respiratory infections. "God has many hands"—and one of them is the angel of the waters. And water, as St. Francis said, is "very serviceable to us."

If God has given healing power to water, then here is reason why man must be concerned about his environment—and his world. Archaeologists believe that society's efforts to manage the water supply were responsible for early developments in government. When the tomb of Cheops was opened, attention was centered upon a boat found there. This was a ship upon which to sail in the realm of departed spirits, and suggests how water dominated all the life of Egypt. The Nile was the one line of communication, and the inhabitants of the valley considered boats the only way to travel, here or hereafter. For them, too, water determined the calendar. The year began with the rapid rising of the Nile. The home of Osiris was in the fresh-water ocean of the underworld, and her dying and rising again were symbolic of how the Nile flooded all vegetation and then subsided, so that life could begin anew.

People in Bible lands have not been so fortunate. Some years ago the city of New York was threatened with a water shortage, its distant reservoirs—far from the city—being reduced to something less than 40 per cent of normal. It was then disclosed that the daily per capita consumption of water in the metropolis was 75 gallons. It was believed that by careful economies this could be reduced to 50. At almost precisely the same time, during the Arab siege of Jerusalem, water within the holy city was rationed at two cups per day per person for all uses.

Americans have been blessed above most people in the abundance of the water supply. Yet careless usage has in some sections of the nation already brought scarcity, and scientists agree that our future population cannot be sure of having water whenever and wherever it is wanted. Seven states in the Great Plains and Southwest have already experienced serious shortage. There is an old Hebrew proverb to the effect that "Water is the least valued among things existing and the most valued among things wanted." The Scripture contains one story about a foreigner who was contemptuous of the water supply in the land of the Hebrews.

10. The Waters of Abana

One has read of a woman who, dissatisfied with advice received from one physician, went to another doctor. "What you need," he said, "is deep inhalations of pure ozone. Come here to my office twice a week, and the treatments will cost you ten dollars apiece." "I knew that other doctor didn't know what he was talking about," she exclaimed. "He said all I needed was just to breathe fresh air." This story comes to mind when we read about treatment which an ancient prophet prescribed for a sick soldier. In 2 Kings (5.1) we read that "Naaman, commander of the army of the king of Syria . . . was a mighty man of valor, but he was a leper."

Naaman's wife had as servant "a little maid from the land of Israel," carried off on one of the raids the Syrians were in the habit of making. Although a foreigner, the maid's humanitarian feeling triumphed over national and social barriers and she made a suggestion regarding her master's health. She knew of a prophet back in the homeland who "would cure him of his leprosy" (2 Kings 5.3). The matter thereupon became one of international protocol. The King of Syria sent a letter to the King of Israel, asking that everything possible be done to restore his general's health. Naaman, on his part, brought with him gifts appropriate to so princely an undertaking: "Ten talents of silver, six thousand shekels of gold, and ten festal garments" (2 Kings 5.5). Apart from the worth of the clothing, this is said to be a sum equivalent to $80,000.

The King of Israel suspected a plot. He knew nothing that would cure ailing foreigners. Failing to cure his rival's army commander, would he open himself to attack? Was this a bit of international intrigue designed to make him fall into the hands of his enemy? But the prophet Elisha came to his rescue and asked the King to send Naaman to him. Naaman's horses and chariots drew up in front of the prophet's door. "Elisha sent a messenger to him, saying, 'Go and wash in the Jordan seven times, and your flesh shall be restored, and you shall be clean'" (2 Kings 5.10). This angered Naaman on two counts, and he stalked away in disgust. It wounded both his pride and sense of propriety. He thought that for so important a personage as himself the prophet would surely have come out personally and not merely communicate with him by messenger. In the second place, it seemed a trivial and inconsequential treatment which the prophet prescribed.

"Behold," he said (2 Kings 5.11 f), "I thought that he would surely come out to me, and stand, and call on the name of the LORD his God, and wave his hand over the place, and cure the leper. Are not Abana and Pharpar, the rivers of Damascus, better than all the waters of Israel?" To all outward appearance, they were infinitely better. Compared with some of the streams of earth, the Jordan is not much of a river. George Adam Smith says: "Mostly silent and black in spite of its speed, but now and then breaking into praise and whitening into foam, Jordan scours along, muddy between banks of mud, careless of beauty, careless of life."

Abana and Pharpar, on the other hand, were clear mountain streams. The former, coming down from Anti-Lebanon, flows through Damascus in seven streams, making the city so verdant that Mohammed, centuries later, refused to enter it since he was not yet ready for Paradise. The Pharpar, descending from Mt. Hermon, flows by Damascus on the south. Since there are such good streams at home, Naaman asks (2 Kings 5.12), " 'Could I not wash in them and be clean?' So he turned and went away in a rage." Members of his retinue gave better advice.

"My father," they said, "if the prophet had commanded you to do some great thing, would you not have done it? How much rather, then, when he says to you, 'Wash, and be clean?' " So he went down and dipped himself seven times in the Jordan, according to the word of the man of God; and his flesh was restored like the flesh of a little child, and he was clean (2 Kings 5.13-15). The ancient world believed in the healing power of running streams. This method of effecting a cure is paralleled in the ancient monuments. In an inscription dating from the age of Sargon, the king of Akkad who flourished around 2800 B.C., Merodach is represented as asking his father Hea how to cure a sick man. Hea replies that the sick man must go and bathe in the sacred waters at the mouth of the Euphrates.

In any case, the Scriptural story of Naaman's cure suggests that people who ask that something great and spectacular be done for them could really be helped by paying attention to little things. In our Lord's own day people were continuously asking for some startling dramatic proof that in him God's healing power really was at work. "What sign do you give?" they were always saying (Mt. 12.38; 16.1; 24.3; Mark 8.11, etc.). Jesus steadily refused to offer any sign. "An evil and adulterous generation," he said (Mt. 16.4), "seeks for a sign." When John the Baptizer, languishing in prison, asked for a sign, Jesus' reply was: "Go and tell John what you hear and see: the blind receive their sight and the lame walk, lepers are cleansed and the deaf hear, and the dead are raised up, and the poor have good news preached to them" (Mt. 11.5).

Jesus' unwillingness to rely on the sensational was dramatized in his temptation experience. The people would have liked him to solve all their problems in spectacular fashion: they wanted him to turn stones into bread. He taught, instead, about God who sends rain from heaven and causes the seed to grow. They wanted him to leap from the pinnacle of the temple. He chose to go about doing good. They wanted him to accept a kingly crown. He adopted the servant's role.

One of his parables, too, condemns our human hankering for some overpowering sign, some overwhelming evidence. The parable of the rich man and Lazarus is concerned with this, rather than with the geography of the afterlife and the temperature of hell. The rich man's heedlessness of human suffering had made for him a private hell. Not all human concern is gone, however. Though careless of strangers, he still is mindful of his brothers. He does not want them to experience what he is experiencing, and is eager to have them warned in time.

He asks, therefore, that Lazarus be sent to his father's house with stern warning for his five brothers. But this would do no good: "They have Moses and the prophets; let them hear them" (Luke 16.29). But everybody has that! The rich man thinks his brothers need something special. But if they do not act upon the basis of what they already know, there is no hope that a specter would frighten them into being good: "If they do not hear Moses and the prophets, neither will they be convinced if some one should rise from the dead" (Luke 16:31).

For our conduct, there is always the example of our dear ones, the voice of conscience, the confidence of those who trust us. If we will not heed those, we can hardly expect God to warn us with a thunderbolt when we are tempted to do wrong. So in the physical realm the earth is richly furnished with things needful for us. Of this, salt is an example. It is one of the most necessary items to sustain us—and it exists in the greatest abundance. It is found on all continents and nearly all countries; fresh supplies are still being discovered. The value of this basic commodity is reflected in the economy and vocabulary of many lands.

In some parts of the world salt is still used as money. Governments have manipulated the salt supply in order to further political aims. When the poor in eighteenth-century France tried to produce salt by evaporating sea water, they were tortured and imprisoned—and hanged for a second offense. This abuse helped stir up the French Revolution. In 1930 Gandhi led a revolt against the salt tax in India. In Kansas there is a city called Salinas, and in Missouri a county called Saline. Salinas were salt-licks. The word "salary" is the Latin *salarius,* derived from "sal," the word for salt. Salarius was the money given to Roman soldiers for salt. Salary is salt money. Hence the expression, "Not worth his salt."

This common product, technically called sodium chloride, has power to cleanse and heal but many are scornful of so humble an agent. Some dentists believe that salt is as good a dentifrice as there is—but Americans must have flavor. And the cleansing power of a dentifrice is not as important as the patina it leaves. Some doctors suggest that in certain throat conditions salt and soda, mixed in water, make as good a gargle as any—but Americans like odoriferous compounds packaged expensively. "Are not Abana and Pharpar, the rivers of Damascus, better than all the waters of Israel?" Naaman's question reflects the mood of twentieth-century Americans, who go for the sensational and the spectacular.

Salesmen assure the restaurant owner that what he really needs to sell is the sizzle, not the steak. If a breakfast food will only crackle there is little need to be concerned with its nutritional value. Soap is to be judged by its smell. Some merchants, playing on our vanity, tell us they do not want our business unless we are prepared to pay enough to get the best. An automobile dealer says that the resale value of an automobile depends upon the kind of radio it has, and has no relation whatever to the condition of the motor.

The doctor's outer office has no connection with his ability at diagnosis or his skill in curing. Some doctors report that a more impressive waiting room enables them to charge higher fees. Women would rather pay for expensive reducing treatments than eat a balanced diet. Men would rather join a health club than be content with salad for lunch. Dr. C. F. Menninger, founder of the Menninger Clinic in Topeka (Kans.), has always insisted that many a mental patient could be cured in a barn if the right people were with him. To our age, all agog for the marvelous, the judgment of Naaman's servant still is relevant: "If the prophet had commanded you to do some great thing, would you not have done it? How much rather, then, when he says to you, 'Wash and be clean'?" In simple ways God makes known His love— and for our diseases sometimes provides specific cures. He is the great Pharmacist of the universe!

11. God Made Medicines

About the year 180 B.C. a sage of Jerusalem set down shrewd observations about the life of men and its relationship to God. His work, the largest in Jewish wisdom literature, reminds us of the Book of Proverbs. It is sometimes called the Wisdom of Sirach. Under its Greek name Ecclesiasticus it appears in the Apocrypha. Ecclesiasticus is notable for its appreciation of the part played in our common life by the craftsmen of various occupations. It praises the plowman, "the smith sitting by the anvil," and the potter. Upon such men all of us are dependent:

"Without them a city cannot be established,
    and men can neither sojourn nor live there.
                .   .   .   .
they keep stable the fabric of the world,
and their prayer is in the practice of their trade."
                                        (Eccles. 38.32, 34).

Ecclesiasticus is grateful also for the work of the apothecary and the healing herbs which God causes to grow:

"The Lord created medicines from the earth,
    and a sensible man will not despise them.

By them he heals and takes away pain;
    the pharmacist makes of them a compound"
                                        (Eccles. 38.4, 7, 8).

Recall the various kinds of medicines and medicinal compounds mentioned in the Bible. The author of Ecclesiasticus himself cites as evidence of the healing power of herbs the fact that water was "made sweet with a tree." This no doubt is an allusion to the circumstances described in Exodus (15.23ff). The Hebrews in their wilderness wanderings had gone three days without water. When they found water at last, they could not drink it. It was so bitter that the place was named Marah, meaning Bitterness. Travelers in that region still testify to the ugly taste of the springs found there.

Moses, however, discovered a certain type of tree and "threw it into the water, and the water became sweet" (Ex. 15.23). It was at this place that God promised: "I will put none of the diseases upon you which I put upon the Egyptians; for I am the LORD, your healer" (Ex. 15.26). This is a passage which the rabbis later used in prayers for the blessing of the sick. In 2 Kings (2.21) is described how Elisha purified a spring. He put salt into it, and heard God say: "I have made this water wholesome; henceforth neither death nor miscarriage shall come from it."

The purification of brackish water is still a major problem for those concerned with public health. An engineer responsible for the water supply of a large population in western Pennsylvania says that these Biblical stories have been the inspiration of his life work and actually point the way to the techniques used by him and his fellow engineers. It is their duty to take water which is bitter and polluted by the industrial waste dumped into it and purify it so as to make it available for human consumption. This they do by the addition of proper chemicals—and salt still plays its part.

Isaiah (38.21) mentions yet another kind of medication. When King Hezekiah was sick, God's spokesman said: "Let them take a cake of figs, and apply it to the boil, that he may recover." If we ask why a prophet should issue such a prescription, the answer is that some medical knowledge was a part of the education of prophet-priests. Among the Greeks, Aesculapius was the god of healing, and temples were erected to him in many communities. The priests of Aesculapius not only presided over worship of the deity but they also offered medical treatment, including baths and massage, to the sick. So also in Israel, there were some diseases especially with which the religious authorities were to deal. Isaiah is God's representative, yet he does not scorn the use of natural remedies, and so orders for the king "a cake of figs."

Here is the type of external application which we call a poultice. The English word "poultice" is derived from "pulse," a term once used for the edible seeds of such plants as beans and peas. In the King James Bible we read how Daniel, rebelling against the extravagances of the court where he was held prisoner, challenged the king to let the young Hebrews have only "pulse to eat, and water to drink" (Dan. 1.12, 16). The REVISED STANDARD VERSION here reads: "vegetables to eat and water to drink."

"Poultice" is used to describe a soft composition of beans or herbs applied to a sore or inflamed part of the body to provide warmth or moisture, or to act as antiseptic or counter-irritant. Figs were believed to have some value in this way, and so a poultice of figs was prescribed for the king's affliction. It is interesting that in the manuscript of the prophet Isaiah, found in the Dead Sea Cave in 1947, a manuscript thought to date from about 100 B.C., this story is found in the margin. The scribe evidently left it out and then inserted it so it would not get lost. This passage in any case seems originally to have been a note on verse 8, supplied from the narrative in 2 Kings 20. It is the kind of thing which in the present day would be put into a footnote.

The poultice reminds us that the Hebrews used other forms of external treatment in the cure of disease. Naaman the

Syrian "was a mighty man of valor, but he was a leper" (2 Kings 5.1). He came to Elijah for healing, and supposed the prophet would do something magical: "Wave his hand over the place, and cure the leper" (2 Kings 5.11). Elijah required him instead to go and bathe seven times in the river Jordan. Francis of Assisi sang of "our sister water," who is "very serviceable to us." A doctor has written that "a cloth wrung out of cold water" can sometimes be used in the relief of pain. At other times the hot-water bottle brings comfort.

Saliva, which initiates the process of digestion, is a part of the body's defense against disease. By the ancients it was believed to have curative power. Three times in the Gospels Jesus is reported to have used it. There was a deaf man who also had an impediment in his speech. Jesus "put his fingers into his ears, and he spat and touched his tongue" (Mark 7.33). The blind man of Bethesda Jesus took "by the hand, and led him out of the village; and when he had spit on his eyes and laid his hands upon him, he asked him, 'Do you see anything?'" (Mark 8.23).

John (9.6f) reveals how Jesus combined the use of spittle with bathing in curative waters. When there was brought to him "a man blind from his birth . . . he spat on the ground and made clay of the spittle and anointed the man's eyes with the clay, saying to him, 'Go, wash in the pool of Siloam.'" In twentieth-century man, cancer of the lung has become much more prevalent, but cancer of the mouth has not. Some researchers believe this is due to the protective power of saliva.

The prophet Ezekiel, encouraging his people who are to return from exile, has a vision in which there appears to him the river of the Hebrew homeland. Beside it healing herbs will grow. "And on the banks, on both sides of the river, there will grow all kinds of trees for food. Their leaves will not wither nor their fruit fail, but they will bear fresh fruit every month, because the water for them flows from the sanctuary. Their fruit will be for food, and their leaves for healing" (Ezek. 47.12). It is impressive to think of what the author of Revelation does with this passage. He, too, has a vision of a river and of life-giving herbs growing on its banks: "Then he showed me the river of the water of life, bright as crystal, flowing from the throne of God and of the Lamb through the middle of the street of the city; also, on either side of the river, the tree of life with its twelve kinds of fruit, yielding its fruit each month; and the leaves of the tree were for the healing of the nations" (Rev. 22.1f).

This is from the last chapter of the last book in the Bible. We have seen that it was in the period between the Testaments that the author of Ecclesiasticus wrote: "The Lord created medicines from the earth." It thus appears that at almost every period of Holy History the writers speak of herbs that bring healing: Moses in the wilderness wanderings, Isaiah in the prophetic era, Ezekiel at the time of the exile, Ben Sirach between the Testaments, the author of Revelation near the end of the first century A.D. It is clear that Scripture places a high value upon the pharmacist and encourages the sick in the use of medicines.

The reason for this becomes apparent in the Ezekiel and Revelation passages just cited. In Ezekiel, the leaves of the tree have therapeutic value because they are nourished by water that "flows from the sanctuary." In Revelation, the healing is present because the water flows "from the throne of God." In other words, the curative power of drugs is traced to its origin in God's own provision for His creation. We think and speak about herbs as natural remedies. The Hebrews did not make the distinction we make between nature and spirit. For them, drugs represented one of the spiritual influences which God has bestowed upon man.

It is impressive to remember how the men of the Bible, in pre-scientific days, made use of these remedies. It is marvelous also to contemplate what new insights God has given the medical profession about the curative power of things that grow. Dr. Alexander Fleming noticed how the staphylococci faded away when a mold called *pencillium notatum* developed on a culture plate—and thus penicillin became available to man. Dr. Selman A. Waksman, studying microorganisms that inhabited New Jersey soil, discovered a fungus that offered natural combativeness to bacteria—and so streptomycin has been added to the antibiotics.

The twentieth century thus can appreciate anew the words of Ecclesiasticus:

> "The Lord created medicines from the earth,
> and a sensible man will not despise them."

Not all medicines, though, are derived from the earth. The Scripture speaks of yet another kind.

12. *This, Too, Is Medicine*

The Bible makes frequent mention of herbs which God has caused to grow for the relief of man's pain and the healing of his disease. It makes much, also, of another kind of medicine. Proverbs (17.22) tells us that

> "A cheerful heart is a good medicine,
> but a downcast spirit dries up the bones."

A cheerful heart is the kind of medicine which is both preventive and cure. To possess it is to have a certain immunity to the woes and worries which make us an easy prey of disease. If we are ill, then a cheerful disposition will enable us to cooperate with the physician in his ministry for our recovery. Conversely, an attitude of gloom will not only incline us to illness but will retard our return to health. In the New Testament this is summed up in Philippians (4.4): "Rejoice in the Lord always; again, I will say, Rejoice."

Isaiah (61.3) speaks of God as one who promises

> "to those who mourn in Zion—
> to give them a garland instead of ashes,
> the oil of gladness instead of mourning,
> the mantle of praise instead of a faint spirit."

Indeed, it could be contended that one characteristic of the God of the Bible is that He is always chasing away deep gloom with laughter. To the disconsolate Job the promise is made (8.21) that God

> "will yet fill your mouth with laughter,
> and your lips with shouting."

The returning exiles enjoyed such a time and celebrated it ever after in song:

> "When the Lord restored the fortunes of Zion,
> we were like those who dream.
> Then our mouth was filled with laughter,
> and our tongue with shouts of joy"
>   (Psalm 126:1f).

Note that the cheerful heart which is a good medicine is not a superficial wise-cracking attitude of irresponsibility. Ecclesiastes (7.6) says:

> "as the crackling of the thorns under a pot,
> so is the laughter of the fools."

In the Hebrew here there is a play on words, that some have rendered: "As crackling nettles under kettles" or "As crackling stubble makes the pot bubble." The picture is of a fire that does not last. Travelers spending the night on Mt. Herman wanted to keep themselves warm. The only fuel to be found high on the mountainside were dried thorn bushes. A pile of them was gathered and ignited. It burst into a roaring flame that soon exhausted itself. Paul says that "fire will test what sort of work each has done" (1 Cor. 3.13). If it is "wood, hay, stubble," it will be quickly consumed. This is in contrast with the more substantial fuel of Bible lands. Attendants at the court of the high priest warmed themselves at "a charcoal fire" (John 18.18). Jesus and his friends, on a post-resurrection morning, ate fish broiled on "a charcoal fire" (John 21:9).

There is nothing substantial, though, about a fire of thorns. It makes a big puff and is gone for ever. So is it with the laughter of fools. It is a crackling that is gone with the instant. The cheerful heart is of a very different order. It is not on the surface, but is deep down in the true nature and disposition. It does not try to pass off difficulties in a Pollyanna sort of way, determined to find something lighthearted in every situation. It is rooted rather in one's confidence that God has a purpose for life which may be achieved in spite of pain and sickness, suffering and sorrow. Paul urges that we rejoice and give thanks, not for all things—this plainly would be the lightheartedness of a fool—but "in all circumstances" (1 Thess. 5.18f).

The Negro has given to the world a remarkable demonstration of what it means to rejoice and give thanks in all circumstances. One of his most marked characteristics is cheerfulness and good spirits. This he has developed, not because success and good fortune have attended his efforts, but quite the other way around. Subjected to slavery and countless other indignities, he has not become bitter nor tried to retaliate in kind. He has known that nothing can cure a broken spirit except a cheerful heart. Perhaps something similar is to be seen in the Jewish people. Is this why they have produced so many of the people who provide us with merriment and relaxation? When Fanny Brice died, the rabbi who conducted her funeral said she had "inherited from the tradition of her people the ability of moving people to tears and laughter. This was because of the tragedy of Jewish life. The jokes, the laughter, were a defence against the barbs of the world."

The therapeutic value of the cheerful heart is recognized by the medical profession. A group of nurses in a mission hospital were discussing the marks of a Christian personality. Faith and love and willingness to serve were high on the list. A significant place also was given to the kind of medicine of which we are thinking. "We decided," wrote one, "that no matter what the circumstances, a smile three times a day and at bedtime should be a minimum in a Christian hospital. We also advised a standing order for extras to be given whenever circumstances should demand."

A children's doctor had an old-fashioned gold watch with a heavy case, the lid of which would fly open at a touch. Wishing to count the pulse, he would hold the closed watch up to the mouth of the child, telling him to blow on it, at the same time releasing the catch so that it would fly open. This was the kind of playfulness which enabled him to win the confidence of young patients. Sir William Osler was always writing notes to sick children, telling them of what he had seen at the zoo, or the latest doings of Katamount, King of the Kats. At night he would whisper in the nursery: "Blessings on you, don't be afraid. Your own doctor loves you and all will be well." An adult said of him: "no human being ever left him disheartened. Those who entered his door in despair left it in hope."

In order to be able to meet our needs instantly, druggists have to carry in store quantities of drugs that may be seldom used, and the high cost of medicine is one of the economic problems of our time. But here is a medicine which involves no expenditure of money and is freely available to all in unlimited quantity. The only price we have to pay is the renunciation of pride and the willingness to see ourselves for what we truly are. A theologian points out how laughter follows repentance. "It is the laughter of those who have been released both from the tyranny of the law and from the slavery of pretending to be better than they are." A philosopher contends that "laughter of any sort may be considered a religious exercise, for it bears witness to the soul's emancipation."

When the history of race relations is written in America, it will have to be recorded that baseball broke the color line before some churches did. Jackie Robinson will be remembered as the first Negro to play in the major leagues. Branch Rickey, a Methodist layman, prepared carefully for his coming. An able player, Robinson became famous up and down the land and climaxed his career by stealing home during a World Series game at the Yankee Stadium in 1955. Robinson, a college graduate, has always had a wholesome concern for the underprivileged, and is frequently called upon to speak at community meetings or on radio and television programs concerned with delinquency and other problems of our society.

In spite of the heights to which his career has carried him, "Robbie" has always maintained a modest bearing. This is probably due to his ability to laugh at himself. Among the many honors that have fallen to him was an honorary degree of doctor of laws, bestowed by Bethune-Cookman College, of

Daytona Beach, Fla. His team-mates in spring training were teasing him about having become a Doctor of Laws. In the batting-cage Duke Snider said to him: "Swing with a little more dignity, doctor." "Wanna know something?" asked Robbie. "I just discovered it hasn't improved my hitting a bit."

On an April day in 1778, two friends who had not seen each other for forty years met outside the Church of St. Clement Danes, in the Strand, London. One was Dr. Samuel Johnson whose literary works include poetry, essays, and a dictionary of the English language, and whose life is well known through Boswell's meticulous study. Of the other we know nothing except that his name was Oliver Edwards and that at his meeting with Johnson he exclaimed: "You, sir, are a philosopher. I too have tried in my time to be a philosopher; but I do not know how—cheerfulness was always breaking in." He who carries about with him the good medicine of a cheerful heart will find that it brings relief in time of tension.

At a critical moment in our national life, the President and his Cabinet were seated solemnly around a table in Washington, awed by the responsibilities facing them. Instead of addressing himself immediately to the business in hand, the President picked up a book and began to read aloud a chapter from a nineteenth century humorist, Artemus Ward. The reading was frequently interrupted by chuckles, but these came only from the President. The Secretaries were shocked. "Gentlemen," asked the President, "why don't you laugh? If I didn't laugh under the strain that is upon me day and night, I should go mad. And you need that medicine as well as I."

So saying, he turned to his tall hat, and drew forth what one of the Cabinet members described as "a little white paper." The President was Abraham Lincoln. The "little white paper" was the emancipation proclamation. This type of therapy is good for us also in the home. A child psychologist declares that a good laugh together at a family joke will do more to improve parent-child relations than a hundred parental scoldings.

The church, presumably, consists of people who live by the Bible. Yet the healing power of holy laughter has been strangely lacking in organized religion. Joking was frowned upon in the monasteries of the middle ages, and from this aspect of medieval times the Reformers did not wholly free themselves. The Directory for Worship of one of our leading denominations provides that at the appointed hour the people are to "enter the church, and take their seats in a decent, grave, and reverent manner." They are to "abstain from all whisperings; from salutations of persons present, or coming in; and from gazing about, sleeping, smiling, and all other indecent behaviour."

Happily, however, not all churchmen have regarded smiling in church as indecent behaviour, and against that view some preachers have entered their protest. Robert South, a seventeenth-century Anglican whose "Sermons Preached Upon Several Occasions" are still read, once observed that "Piety engages no man to be dull, though lately, I confess, dullness with some is taken for a mark of regeneration."

In the summer of 1950 Baron Mountevans told the British House of Lords that twentieth century religion was suffering from a lack of humor. He suggested that there was need for a revision of the prayers conventionally used in church. This he offered as a sample of the kind that was needed:

> "God, give me sympathy and common sense,
>   And help me home with courage high.
>   God, give me calm and confidence
>   And please—a twinkle in my eye."

For our healing, God has provided nurses and medicines and laughter—and physicians, too.

13. The Good Physician

It is said that on the parapet of a bridge leading to an Austrian city there are twelve statues of Christ, each representing him in a different capacity. One shows him as the prophet, another as the priest, another as king. One represents him as a sower, another as a carpenter, another as a physician. Each of these representations has a special appeal to one group or another. Early in the morning, the farmer, on his way to market with his produce, pauses before Christ the sower. A little later, the artisan, on his way to work in the city, pays tribute to Christ the carpenter. Later still, the invalid, creeping toward town for medical aid, prays to Christ the physician.

Christ does have something in common with all sorts of people, and perhaps for us in the twentieth century, none of his roles is more compelling that that of Good Physician. One of his sayings revealed how he thought of himself in this relationship: "Those who are well," he said (Mark 2.17), "have no need of a physician, but those who are sick; I came not to call the righteous, but sinners." Jesus always speaks of those in distress as the objects of God's gracious concern. His attention is fixed upon the one lost sheep rather than upon the ninety-nine who are safe within the fold. His heart goes out, not to the elder brother who has security at home, but to the one lost in the far country.

Luke the physician alone remembered a parable that pictured God's searching love in terms of healing. When he found a man beaten and wounded, the Good Samaritan "bound up his wounds, pouring on oil and wine" (Luke

10.34). This man also gave of himself to be sure that other needed attention would be available for the sufferer: "he set him on his own beast and brought him to an inn, and took care of him" (Luke 10.34). Isaiah (40.11) pictures the Good Shepherd:

> "He will gather the lambs in his arms,
> he will carry them in his bosom,
>   and gently lead those that are with young."

These aspects of God's care for His people stress the outgoing nature of the love which the Good Physician has: he goes out in search of the afflicted. Sometimes even in a great city a doctor is hard to get. He may have gone on his boat for the week-end. He may be at his summer place. He may have slipped away to the football game. No one begrudges him his rest and recreation. Without these he could not carry on at all. Some doctors practice in partnership, so that one will always be available.

At best, the ordinary physician waits to be summoned. We cannot expect him to anticipate our situation and simply show up when needed. But the Good Physician does not have to be sent for. He is always on the lookout for those who need him. The worse our plight, the more eager he is to help. When sin has done its worst to us, we are apt to suppose that God has cut us off. But this is just exactly when He wants to help. He is most near when most needed. It is the Good Physician who says: "I came not to call the righteous, but sinners." The Jewish commentator, C. G. Montefiore, calls this "a new and sublime contribution to the development of religion and morality."

Jesus not only calls us, but gives of himself to make us well. A missionary doctor among the Arabs found a lad who needed a blood transfusion, and suggested that some member of the family be chosen as donor. The group, however, was not familiar with the techniques of scientific medicine, and none was willing. The doctor thereupon opened his own veins and gave the sick boy the needed life fluid. The family was profoundly impressed, and when the boy got well they boasted of the doctor: "He is one of us now—his blood is in our veins."

Plainly, the physician cannot often respond in that fashion. But the Good Physician can and does. Among Old Testament passages which influenced Jesus, none had a greater effect than the 53rd chapter of Isaiah. This represents the Messiah as voluntary sharer in our woe, as completely identifying himself with our race:

> "he was wounded for our transgressions,
>   he was bruised for our iniquities;
> upon him was the chastisement that made us whole,
>   and with his stripes we are healed."

The Good Physician does not wait to be summoned. He not only calls the patient, but gives of himself for the patient's healing. Yet another characteristic of the Good Physician must not be overlooked. When Alexander Woollcott was in his last illness, he said to Lillian Gish:

> "Doctors want to keep you alive; I want to live."

Twentieth century science has made marvelous strides in keeping people alive. The Psalmist wrote long ago:

> "The years of our life are threescore and ten,
>   or even by reason of strength fourscore" (Psalm 90:10).

This was a reference to the maximum human age rather than to the average. It has remained for our era to see life expectancy raised almost to the Biblical maximum. Since 1950, life expectancy in the United States has risen from 48 years to 69.8—only a few months short of the Psalmist's 70.

Statisticians tell us that in the Roman Empire at the time of Christ the newborn child could expect to live only 22 years. In the Middle Ages it rose to 35, and the early nineteenth century to 40. Some scientists are now venturing to predict the doubling of human longevity. The life span of fruit flies has been increased by 46 per cent, and some experimenters hold that the same technique can be applied to men and women. A major cause of death is the breakdown of the cardiovascular system, resulting from the deposit of cholesterol in the blood vessels, heart, muscles, and other parts of the body. It is contended that the use of certain chemicals can prevent this. There seems still to be a question regarding just what quantity of these chemicals ought to be administered to human beings at different ages.

The Good Physician, however, is not interested simply in keeping us alive. He wants us to live. In 1934 at a meeting of the Academy of Sciences, in Cleveland, Dr. Wilder Bancroft, a professor of chemistry at Cornell, announced that he was on the trail of a method of extending the mortal span. Experiments already made seemed to indicate that appropriate doses of sodium rhodanate would increase the life of the average person by at least two years. Dr. Bancroft's report of his research was made with enthusiasm, since he regarded himself as a public benefactor. Much to his surprise, some of his colleagues seemed to look upon him rather as a public enemy. Some who took part in the debate held that it would be cruel to prolong man's life in a time when the problems of war and unemployment had not been solved, and anxiety was taking such a heavy toll.

This may very well be our reaction if we think only in terms of extending man's years. Christianity, however, does not think of life in terms of quantity but of quality. It is not a matter of duration but of continually new creation (*see* 2

Cor. 5.17). This life we should be eager for all our fellows to know.

At the Columbia University Centennial, the universities of India were represented by Sir Sarvepalli Radhakrishnan, who said that the contemporary world situation reminded him of a story which circulates in the Orient. Christ came to a certain city and was astonished to discover the condition of persons previously healed by him. He saw a young man lying drunk on a window sill. "Why do you waste your time in drunkenness?" Jesus asked. The reply was: "Lord, I was a leper, and you healed me: what else can I do?" A little farther along he saw a young man following a harlot. "Why do you dissolve your soul in debauchery?" asked Jesus. The young man answered, "Lord, I was blind and you healed me; what else can I do?"

In still another part of the city he saw an old man, crouched upon the ground, weeping bitterly. When Jesus asked why he wept, the old man replied: "Lord, I was dead, and you restored me to life; what else can I do but weep?" Mere physical life is not enough. "Advances" in modern medicine may not be thought advances unless they are accompanied by opportunities to do something finer and better with the length of days bestowed by science. This was illustrated in a story told long ago by the Greeks, who sometimes reported that gods and goddesses fell in love with mortals.

This happened to Aurora, goddess of the dawn. Her favorite was Tithonus, son of Laomedon, king of Troy. She stole him away, and was so eager to enjoy the delights of love for ever that she prevailed upon Zeus to grant him immortality. She forgot to ask, however, that youth accompany the gift of everlastingness. To her great sorrow, she soon began to discover that her lover was growing old. When his hair turned white, she refused to have anything more to do with him, but he continued to live on in her palace, clad in celestial raiment and dining on ambrosial food. When at length he lost the power of using his limbs, she shut him up in his chamber, whence his feeble voice might at times be heard.

Tennyson in one of his poems pictures the helpless old man as asking the gods to take back their gift. He describes how the elements in nature are permitted to decay:

> "And after many a summer dies the swan.
> Me only cruel immortality
> consumes."

He speaks of himself as "this gray shadow, once a man," condemned

> "To dwell in presence of immortal youth,
> Immortal age beside immortal youth,
> And all I was, in ashes."

Unending life he regards as a curse and speaks

> "Of happy men that have the power to die."

The Greek legend had it that Aurora, who could no longer endure the sight of her lover grown so aged and infirm, turned him into a grasshopper. This suggests how shriveled and meaningless life may become if it holds nothing more than longevity. In such a world we need the help of him who said: "Those who are well have no need of a physician, but those who are sick. I came not to call the righteous, but sinners."

II. SOUL

14. *Health Is Wholeness*

Before psychosomatic medicine had become a part of the doctor's training, Dr. C. F. Menninger, a horse-and-buggy doctor in Kansas, did not lightly dismiss patients whose aches in back, head, stomach, limb, or heart seemed to have no organic cause. He concluded rather that "their physical complaints were merely roundabout efforts to communicate to me their emotional needs." It was this conviction which led to the establishment in Topeka of the Menninger Clinic. One of the brief letters of John gives Scriptural expression to the truth derived by Dr. Menninger from his practice: "Beloved, I pray that all may go well with you and that you may be in health, as I know it is well with your soul" (3 John 2).

A professor in the Johns Hopkins School of Medicine reported that approximately one-third of all victims of tuberculosis also had serious problems of non-physical character. "In a surprisingly large number of patients," he said, "it will eventually be seen that falling ill with tuberculosis was a way of attempting to escape from an unbearable emotional situation." He cited the case of one tuberculosis patient who had recovered quickly after his mother-in-law died. She had lived in his home. Her own illness, self-pity, and incessant complaints had made life so miserable for him that he unconsciously concluded that life in a sanitarium would be more bearable than life at home.

The English poet Philip James Bailey seems to be the authority for the statement that beauty is "but skin deep." For all those not blessed with attractive features or normal pigmentation this may be genuine consolation. In spite of what they happen to look like on the outside, they will be able to cultivate what I Peter (3:4) describes as "the hidden person of the heart, with the imperishable jewel of a gentle and quiet spirit." In view, however, of the close relationship between soul and body, it may be that the "gentle and quiet spirit" within may manifest itself in the outward appearance. The skin responds to emotion just as much as the stomach or the heart. Some effects of the emotions upon the skin, such as blushing, are transient; others may become chronic.

A German dermatologist, Dr. Eugene Traugott Bernstein, says that emotions make their impact upon the skin first by disturbing the sympathetic nervous system, then the blood vessels, muscles, and nutrition of the skin itself. Reactions of this sort may become a kind of bad habit. A young lady was subject to the most vicious attacks of hives. And they always came at the wrong time: just before she was to take part in some public event, just before an important date with a boyfriend. Invariably the hour of the great occasion would find her incapacitated, and her participation had to be called off.

She had been orphaned quite early in life, and had been brought up by her grandmother and a bachelor uncle. Suspecting some correlation between emotional tension and the skin eruptions, her pastor took occasion one day to have a long talk with her, reassuring her about her own gifts of personality, so that she had no need to feel inferior, and seeking to awaken in her an awareness of the contribution she might make to the lives of others. Hives did not develop for the big date she was to have that week-end. Instead, she became engaged and shortly afterwards was happily married. So far as is known, there has never been a recurrence of the hives. A well-attested phenomenon in the lives of the mystics is the bleeding of hands and feet, chest and forehead, in a pattern corresponding to the wounds Christ suffered at his crucifixion. Students of skin conditions believe that this is a hysterical outward manifestation of an inner attempt of the sufferer to identify himself with Christ.

Headache may be the beginning of a serious ailment. Or, it may have no physical basis at all and simply result from psychogenic factors. Analyzing various types of headaches, Dr. Noah D. Fabricant said that human beings "can be thrown off balance by emotions such as hate, hostility, anger, rage, resentment, jealousy, and suspicion. Professional men, business executives and white-collar workers are vulnerable to psychogenic headaches, which are likely to put in appearance at the end of a trying day." Sometimes the inciting cause may be an unhappy combination of external circumstances; more often, perhaps, it is something in the inner life of the sufferer which prevents adequate adjustment to the ordinary demands of daily life. Headaches of this kind may not follow any pattern as to time, location, or duration of the pain.

Physical pain can also be induced by wrong attitudes or disposition. A doctor at the Veterans Administration Mental Clinic in Boston studied 52 men, half of whom were subject to migraine headaches. All were subjected to unpleasant situations. Measurements of muscle tension and heart rates showed that the migraine sufferers showed greater physiological strain than the others but would say less about it. The conclusion was that migraine headaches may result from a feeling of hostility coupled with inability to express hostility in any other way.

That pain owes part of its intensity to our attitude toward it is clearly indicated by the fact that soldiers and civilians react differently to injuries that might be quite similar. A doctor who, during the Second World War, spent 75 days on the Anzio beachhead, says: "Of the badly wounded men I examined on the beachhead, only one man in four asked for relief from pain. On the other hand, when a similar group of civilians are treated for wounds, three out of four experience great pain. This is a mental process." To the soldier, a wound means escape from battle, the comfort of a hospital bed, rest, and safety. All this he welcomes, and therefore he minimizes the pain. To the civilian, an accident means absence from work, duties piled up at the office, a missed fishing trip. All this he dislikes, and therefore the wound is unbearable.

That pain, in its extent and intensity, is in some degree related to what goes on in the mind is dramatically suggested by the experience of women in childbirth. A study made at the St. Louis Maternity Hospital indicated that women who accepted gladly the role of prospective mother had less nausea during pregnancy, less pain in childbirth, and went through the whole experience with comparatively little difficulty. Women who rebelled against the role had a "stormy" pregnancy and a difficult delivery. It is similar reasoning which leads many obstetricians to believe that a home is a better place than a hospital for a mother to be when her child is born. The hospital is a convenience for the doctor, and sometimes a mother's being there has facilitated emergency treatment without which death might have resulted. On the other hand, as one medical specialist puts it, when obstetric care of the mother was moved to the hospital, "childbearing was transported from the natural, intimate, human atmosphere of the family to the atmosphere of sickness, abnormality, and death which permeate hospital care."

In every community there are couples who, unable to have children of their own, adopt a child, and soon afterwards the supposedly sterile mother has a child of her own. The previous inability to become pregnant was not due at all to "sterility" of the body but rather to factors that were in the mind and spirit. Sometimes the inability factor is a fear of childbearing, sometimes it is unconscious opposition to the inconvenience and discomfort of pregnancy. Once a child has been adopted, however, psychological barriers are lowered, and the normal process of pregnancy is allowed to function without hindrance.

If there is any part of the body not affected by the emotions, it would seem to be the teeth. They are made of a hard substance which would appear impervious to subtle influences. Yet dentists now believe that emotional states produce many significant effects upon the teeth. It begins even before we are born. Maternal anxiety during pregnancy, no less than maternal dietary deficiency during pregnancy, may cause faulty development. Overprotection in childhood may prevent the proper maturation of the teeth one has. Some parents believe that everything in the child's life, including his food, must be softened as much as possible. Such a child is, quite literally, not allowed to get his teeth into anything. The consequent lack of stimulation and disuse result in general softness and poor dentition.

One phase of parental anxiety is a morbid concern lest the child put into his mouth something which does not belong there. The mouth is one of the organs of investigation by means of which the child learns of the world about him. A certain amount of stimulus also is needed in the oral zone. Parents, troubled because nothing they could think of could make their small child stop its thumb-sucking, appealed to the pediatrician. "Don't worry about it," he said. "Just keep his thumb clean!" Constant nagging of children can cause emotional upsets that change the saliva from alkaline to acid almost instantly and lead to gastric upsets, disturbance of the thyroid and other glands, upset the calcium balance, and otherwise affect the child adversely.

Even when teeth are grown, emotional disturbance can have its effect upon denture. One dentist is sure that disappointment in love may cause a young man's teeth to decay in a few months. Sudden tooth decay in the middle-aged almost always reveals that the patient has gone through a period of depression resulting from extra work, added responsibility, or deep anxiety. Realization that man is "body, soul, and spirit" has caused some reconsideration of the focus-of-infection theory. Time was when aches and pains in other parts of the body that could not be accounted for otherwise were attributed to some focus of infection. This might be the tonsils or it might be the teeth. In any case, the thing to do was to get rid of the part that had become suspect. One doctor says that "if we could pile together the teeth and tonsils that have been unnecessarily removed from patients with illnesses of emotional origin, we would have an imposing monument to an era of overcredulity in regard to a significant American contribution to medicine." Since teeth and tonsils have something to do with personality, it is often important to search the life situation for the focus of conflict rather than examine the oral cavity for a focus of infection.

"I pray that all may go well with you and that you may keep well, as I know it is well with your soul." The Greek at this point could be translated, "that you may have a happy journey and be in good health even as your soul has a happy journey." The interdependence here is suggested by a cycle of English words whose relationship is not always remembered. The words, all going back to a common root, are hale, heal, health, whole, holy. To be hale, Webster says, is to be free from defect, disease, or infirmity. To heal is to make hale. One who is hale has health. Health means the state of being sound in body, mind, or soul. To be healthy is to be whole, and to be whole is to be holy. The attainment of this state sometimes requires a serious operation!

15. Gospel Surgery

Remembering that in Europe the barber and the surgeon were once one and the same, we are apt to think of surgery as a branch of medicine which has been wholly developed in the modern world. But the barber-surgeon represented a regression. A cleavage arose between the physician and the surgeon, and surgery was often left to itinerant practitioners, some of whom were charlatans.

Surgery had its beginnings in the ancient world and was known to the men of Bible times. By the introduction of antisepsis, Sir Joseph Lister greatly lowered the mortality rate, yet in the Neolithic age saws of stone and bone were used to perform amputations. Harvey Cushing was a twentieth century doctor through whom brain surgery became a science of its own. Yet in prehistoric times sharpened flints were used to remove circular pieces of the skull to relieve epilepsy and other afflictions.

We speak of God as the Good Physician, yet among the relics surviving from New Testament days are surgical instruments which bear a striking resemblance to those still in use: cautery, scissors, probe, needle, a device for lifting depressed portions of the skull. It need not surprise us, therefore, to find in the Scripture ideas which entitle us to speak also of the Good Surgeon. The Bible knows that it is sometimes necessary to give pain in order to bring healing. In the Song of Moses (Deut. 32.39) God says:

> "I kill and I make alive;
> I wound and I heal."

91

Concerning God's dealings with Egypt, Isaiah (19.22) speaks of the Lord as "smiting and healing, and they will return to the Lord and he will heed their supplications and heal them." In picturing God's gracious care, the same prophet (30.26) looks to "the day when the LORD binds up the hurt of his people, and heals the wound inflicted by his blow." Hosea (6.1), "prophet of the unalterable love of God," is sure that there is pardon for sinful men:

> "Come, let us return to the LORD;
> for he has torn, that he may heal us;
> he has stricken and he will bind us up."

In the vineyards of the world the pruning knife does what the surgeon's scapel does for human bodies. Jesus saw in this also an analogy to the higher life of the spirit: "I am the true vine, and my Father is the vinedresser. Every branch of mine that bears no fruit, he takes away, and every branch that does bear fruit he prunes, that it may bear more fruit" (John 15.1, 2). Both the pruning knife and the surgical scalpel are like a loving father's sure discernment which insists on amputating the putrefactions that could destroy the object of his affection:

> "For the Lord disciplines him whom he loves,
> and chastises every son whom he receives"
>   (Heb. 12.6).

The surgeon's knife is evidence of God's gracious provision for his people, and it is never so effectively wielded as when guided by such sympathy as Christ had for the suffering and afflicted. In an address at Glasgow in 1860, Lord Lister stated "the two great requisites for the medical profession: first, a warm loving heart, and secondly, truth in an earnest spirit." One has sometimes heard of surgeons on shipboard or in faraway countries who operated on themselves. Sur-

geons do not ordinarily do this, but Jesus enjoined upon his
followers the most drastic form of self-amputation: "If your
right eye causes you to sin, pluck it out and throw it away;
it is better that you lose one of your members than your
whole body be thrown into hell. And if your right hand
causes you to sin, cut it off and throw it away; it is better
that you lose one of your members than that your whole
body go into hell" (Mt. 5.29, 30). To this Mark (9.45) adds:
"If your foot causes you to sin, cut it off; it is better for you
to enter life lame than with two feet to be thrown into hell."
Matthew (18.8) gives this summary: "it is better for you to
enter life maimed or lame than with two hands or two feet
to be thrown into the eternal fire."

Jesus is concerned always to emphasize the inwardness of
true religion: "There is nothing outside a man which by
going into him can defile him . . . what comes out of a man
is what defiles a man. For from within, out of the heart of
man, come evil thoughts, fornication, theft, murder, adultery,
coveting, wickedness, deceit, licentiousness, an evil eye,
slander, pride, foolishness. All these evil things come from
within, and they defile a man" (Mk. 7.15, 20-23). If this be
true, what good can possibly come from plucking out eyes,
cutting off hands and feet? Possibly this is Jesus' way of at-
tacking an idea, common in the East and found still in cults
of the West, that matter is itself the seat of moral evil. Some
in our Lord's time refrained from marriage on the ground
that sensual affection lured the soul away from its heavenly
dwelling and imprisoned it in the body.

The New Testament at many places exposes the falsity of
this view, and it may be that that is what Jesus here has in
mind. If you really believe that it is your body which is the
cause of evil, then the less body you have, the better! If
iniquity makes its abode in the flesh, then the man with one
arm, one leg, one eye has less temptation to wrestle with.

But the one remaining eye and arm and leg might still get him into trouble, and so the absurdity of this belief is exposed.

It is more likely, however, that Jesus is picturesquely driving home the truth that life's lesser things must not be allowed to come between us and life's finest things. Sir Isaac Newton claimed that he had been able to formulate the law of gravity only because he had learned to resist all forms of temptation that would have diverted his attention. Paderewski is reported to have said that if he omitted his practice one day, he noticed it; if he omitted it two days, the critics noticed it; if he omitted it three days, the public noticed it.

For causes which men love they are willing to risk life and limb. During the First World War, the French General Henri Joseph Etienne Gouraud was severely wounded at Gallipoli. Both legs and one arm riddled with enemy bullets, he was taken to the hospital. Surgeons told him the arm would heal in three months. The wounded commander asked how soon he could return to the front if the arm were amputated. "Two months," was the answer. "Amputate!" he said. Ignatius Loyola, before he founded the Jesuits, was a Spanish nobleman devoted to military life. During a war with the French he was wounded at the siege of Pamplona. When the shattered bone of his leg healed in such a way as to interfere with his riding into battle, he twice ordered the bones to be broken, and willingly endured this torture in the vain hope that he might once again mount his war horse.

It is not alone devotion to country which can induce men to make such heroic sacrifices. An early tradition regarding the author of our second Gospel speaks of Mark as "the stump-figured one." Various explanations are given for this epithet. One is that in the scuffle the night our Lord was arrested, he not only lost his coat (cf. Mk. 14.51 f) but also had his fingers sheared off by the sword of the arresting officer.

Another is that when he became a Christian he deliberately maimed his body by cutting off his thumbs so that he would not have to serve as a priest and would be free to travel. Another is that he found his hand a source of temptation and chopped it off in literal obedience to our Lord's command.

In the tumultuous days of the Protestant Reformation, Thomas Cranmer was one of England's heroes. It was he who placed an English translation of the Bible in the churches. His litany was incorporated in the book of Common Prayer. He lent important doctrinal guidance to the church of England. In the reaction under Bloody Mary, he was condemned as a traitor. Facing a terrible death, he recanted. Fastened to the stake, he was asked to recant publicly. But in the end he saw his way so clearly that he held his hand, which had earlier signed the recantation, in the fire until it was consumed. "In that magnificent gesture," says Trevelyan, "the Church of England revived."

When the French under Napoleon invaded Russia, they came to one village whence all the inhabitants had fled except one old man who was unwilling to leave the village of his fathers. He lingered near his old home, with no protection save the axe in his belt. The French captured him and ordered that he be shot. So calmly did he face the firing squad that the captain ordered his life to be spared. "But," said he, "we must put a mark on him."

Accordingly, a red hot iron was brought and burned its way through the quivering flesh, deep into the back of his hand. When the iron was removed, there was the letter "N"— he had been branded as cattle are branded on the western plains. "There," said the captain, "that stands for Napoleon; you belong to him now." The old Russian woodsman, thus marked, calmly laid his hand upon a block of wood, took his axe from his belt and cut off his own hand. "There," he exclaimed, "there is no part of me now that does not belong to the Czar." This is the kind of devotion which Christ's cause demands. Whatever gets in the way of our full service to him —even though it be an eye, arm, leg—must be removed by Gospel surgery. Sometimes, too, it is harmful attitudes which must be amputated.

16. Do Not Be Anxious

Is "Age of Anxiety," the ballet by Jerome Robbins, the appropriate artistic expression of modern American life? It is striking that the time of unparalleled material comfort should also be the time of unprecedented disquietude and fearful doubt. Some suppose that the waves of hatred and hysteria which have characterized our era are nothing more nor less than a symptom of our anxiety. An optimist is now defined as some one who says the future is uncertain. Painfully aware that we do not know what it holds, we try to relieve our uneasiness by pouring vituperation upon Democrats, Republicans, Socialists, Capitalists, Communists, labor leaders, Europeans, Asians, Africans.

People in our frantic society take strange ways of trying to forget their anxiety. Edward Young spoke of "Tired nature's sweet restorer, balmy sleep." But those who are greatly troubled find it difficult to avail themselves of this "balm of hurt minds," and so resort to sleeping pills. In a recent year the number of those consumed in our country averaged out to twenty-four per person—and that includes men, women, and children. There are annually a thousand deaths attributed to the excessive use of sleeping pills. This includes suicides and accidental overdoses. Some listed as suicides were simply intoxicated by what they had already taken, and didn't realize what they were doing in gulping more.

In addition to the direct effect, sleeping pills contribute to many other crimes and sorrows. Their first effect may not be immediate drowsiness at all, but instead a relaxation of the inner safeguards against antisocial acts. One authority declares that "Addiction to sleeping pills is far more dangerous to the patient and to society than is heroin addiction. During the period of barbiturate intoxication the user may be far more aggressive, acting out angers and sex behavior, than a heroin addict." In the habitual user, brain and nerves are dulled. Progressive poisoning leads to a coma which may befall while he is at the wheel of an automobile, and a toll of grief and misery will be levied upon yet other families.

To the people of another troubled time—Gilbert Murray says it was an age characterized by the failure of nerve—Jesus said flatly: "do not be anxious about tomorrow" (Mt. 6.34). It is important that we should have a correct translation of this passage. An article in a denominational paper stated that if we were to take Jesus seriously we should never purchase any insurance—did he not say, "Take no thought for the morrow"?

A veteran of the First World War did follow this injunction with exact literalness and great enthusiasm. His existence had always been on the level of bare subsistence. Immediately upon the receipt of his bonus, he made a great splurge: bought an automobile, moved to a more expensive part of town, stocked his house with new furniture. Within three months he was back again in poverty. Is this the kind of conduct Jesus would commend? If he ever said, "Take no thought for the morrow," he was being strangely inconsistent. We find him regularly practicing foresight. When his journey to Jerusalem was in prospect, he sent out disciples to prepare the way (Luke 9.51, 52).

Arrangements were evidently made in advance for his use of a donkey for the entry into the city (Mk. 11.1-7), and of a room for the Last Supper (Mk. 14.12-16). The message he sent to Herod indicated that he had a carefully laid out plan for the days immediately ahead: "Go and tell that fox, 'Behold, I cast out demons and perform cures today and tomorrow, and the third day I finish my course. Nevertheless I must go on my way today and tomorrow and the day following" (Luke 13.32f). Jesus did not face tomorrow carelessly.

His teaching also inculcates a wise foresight. He holds up to ridicule a man who tried to build a tower without reckoning up in advance what it would cost: "when he has laid a foundation, and is not able to finish, all who see it begin to mock him, saying, 'This man began to build and was not able to finish'" (Luke 14.29f). Jesus commended the prudent overseer not for his harshness but because he was shrewd enough to prepare for the future by making friends while he could (Luke 16.1-9). Jesus warns all his friends to be ready for that day of reckoning whose advent no one can predict (Mt. 24.36, 44).

"Take no thought for the morrow" would be strangely out of keeping with all else that we know of Jesus' teaching and example. "Take no thought for the morrow" is actually a pagan, not a Christian, philosophy. It is Epicureanism. Epicurus was a Greek who lived some 300 years before Christ and held that pleasure was the only good. Nobody knows what will come afterwards, and the only smart thing to do is to seize the present moment. It is the attitude of Omar Khayyam:

> "The Bird of Time has but a little way
> To flutter—and the Bird is on the wing."

The only thing that matters, then is

> "A Book of Verses underneath the Bough,
> A Jug of Wine, a Loaf of Bread—and Thou.
> Ah, my Beloved, fill the Cup that clears
> Today of past Regrets and future fears:
> Tomorrow!—Why, Tomorrow I may be
> Myself with Yesterday's Seven thousand Years."

Although we associate this idea with Epicurus, it was popular in Israel at the time of the Assyrian invasion. To the prophet this was plainly a time for weeping and mourning and girding with sackcloth. What he saw, on the contrary, was

> "slaying oxen and killing sheep,
>   eating flesh and drinking wine.
> 'Let us eat and drink,
>   for tomorrow we die.'" (Is. 22.13)

The prophet heard God's judgment upon such conduct:

> "'Surely this iniquity will not be
>   forgiven you
>   till you die,'
> says the Lord God of hosts."

This attitude was prevalent also among some in the time of the New Testament, and Paul says that, if it were not for the good hopes of the Gospel, that might be the best that anybody could do. "If the dead are not raised, 'Let us eat and drink, for tomorrow we die'" (1 Cor. 15.32).

Unless Jesus has become an Epicurean, we must put it down as a certainty that he did not say: "Take no thought for the morrow." As a matter of fact, this is a place where the changing nature of the English language must be taken into account. We are told that in the seventeenth century "thought" conveyed the sense of "undue care" or "anxiety," so that "Take no thought for the morrow" really meant "Do not be anxious." If so, that was a good translation for its time, but can no longer be thought of as God's word to us. What the Greek here says is: "Do not be over-anxious," "Do not be torn with care, worry, anxiety." The REVISED STANDARD VERSION then is right: "Therefore do not be anxious about tomorrow, for tomorrow will be anxious for itself. Let the day's own trouble be sufficient for the day."

There is no Biblical ground, then, for carelessness in making or keeping appointments, or being indigent in providing for the needs of our household. Insurance is the modern way of sharing risks among large portions of society, and is certainly not forbidden by the Sermon on the Mount. What is forbidden is that carping care about worldly goods which robs a man of sleep, and ultimately puts him on the ulcer route.

A man of fourscore years was striding up the hill to the post office in a North Carolina community. He was carrying some letters to be mailed. They were addressed in a firm, bold hand—that of a man of forty. "That your handwriting?" asked one who had just been introduced to him. "Yes," was the reply. "There is nothing about it or you to suggest that you are eighty." "Never had toothache, earache or headache in my life," he said. "My wife says there is nothing strange about the latter—insists there's nothing in it to ache. And I certainly wouldn't dispute her," he added gleefully, "because I've had her for fifty-six years."

"How about your parents and grandparents?" he was asked "Did they belong to the race of long-livers?" "Not particularly," was the reply. "Then," the new friend inquired, "what is the secret of your preservation down to old age?" "New Testament Greek," was his startling reply. "The King James Version in the sixth chapter of Matthew says, 'Take no thought for the morrow,' but that's not right. You have to take thought for the morrow. What the Greek says is, 'Do not worry about tomorrow.' I said to myself, when I read that in college, 'If God says not to worry, then He must know what He's talking about, and I'm not going to worry.'"

"From that day to this," he went on, "I have never allowed anxiety to enter my life or my home. There are only two kinds of things you can worry about anyway: things you can help and things you can't help. If you can help them, then do something about them and don't worry. If you can't help, then worry will have no effect, and there is no use to engage in it." What difference would it make to us if we took Jesus seriously at this point? "Take no thought for the morrow" is for drunkards and idiots. "Do not be anxious about tomorrow" is the quiet confidence of a child of God. He who has attained this state will be in a better position, too, to handle anger.

17. Be Angry, and Do Not Sin

H. G. Wells was once asked to list the half dozen greatest names in history. One does not give an offhand answer to a question like that, but in a few days the author of the popular "Outline of History" came up with this answer: "Jesus, Buddha, Asoka, Aristotle, Roger Bacon, Abraham Lincoln." Here we have the One who came to "fulfil the law, the prophets and the psalms"; the founder of an Oriental religion; a ruler who turned his back upon war; a Greek thinker; a medieval mystic who combined science and theology; an American president among whose most famous words are: "With malice toward none; with charity for all; with firmness in the right, as God gives us to see the right."

It is significant that Alexander, Caesar, Charlemagne and Napoleon do not figure in the list, which indeed includes no one whose claim to fame rests upon military exploits. Wells' choice strikingly illumines a saying from the wisdom literature of the Hebrews:

"He who is slow to anger is better than the mighty,
    and he who rules his spirit than he who takes a city."
                                                    (Prov. 16.32)

There is indeed a story about how Buddha, in his old age, disturbed by a quarrel with his cousin, attained that mastery over himself which led to his being called the enlightened one.

An African proverb assures us that "Anger is a warmth which lights itself," and ruling his own spirit is a continuing problem for every human being. Failure here will leave its mark upon our bodies and make us the easy victims of disease. Doctors tell us that headache and heart trouble are but two of the symptoms sometimes induced by anger. Here is a place where the relationship between body and soul is apparent to any one who has suddenly had some one step athwart his path and frustrate his earnest endeavor. When anger is kindled, the heart is speeded up, the muscles become taut, the blood rushes to the surface so that our faces turn red. Fatigue disappears, and we find ourselves possessed of unusual energy. This we may want to expend by punching somebody in the nose. A better way is to turn our attention to some form of activity which will help to relieve the situation which induced the anger.

There is a physical basis for all this. In cases of shock, asthma, or hemorrhage, shots of adrenaline are sometimes administered. This is a chemical which accelerates the heartbeat, increases the blood pressure, and speeds up the liver's output of stored sugar. The body has its own plant for manufacturing adrenaline. This consists of yellowish glands about two inches long, resting on the upper part of the kidneys. The secretion from these glands normally oozes slowly into the blood, producing a tonic effect on the heart and muscles. In anger, however, the secretion of these glands is enormously speeded up. All the organs get big doses of it, and some of them are strongly affected by it. On the digestive organs, adrenaline has a retarding effect. The churning movement of the intestine comes to a halt, gastric juice ceases to flow, and digestion stops.

The adrenal glands are ductless. That is to say, whenever their secretion flows, it is released into the bloodstream. There is nowhere else for it to go. It thus becomes clear that if we frequently give way to anger, our digestion is bound to suffer. The old commentator was more of a scientist than he knew when he compared anger to poison. "It can sometimes be used as a medicine," he said, "but must be managed with the utmost caution."

Jesus warned against the mismanagement of anger. In the Sermon on the Mount he recalls how earlier teachers had said: "You shall not kill." Jesus added: "But I say to you that every one who is angry with his brother shall be liable to judgment" (Mt. 5.22). Some versions make this read: "whosoever is angry with his brother without a cause, shall be in danger of the judgment." But it is clear from the ancient manuscripts that "without a cause" was written in by a medieval copyist who felt that some provision ought to be made for righteous indignation. Jesus made no such comfortable exception, and it is sobering to learn that anger always puts us in jeopardy.

Side by side with that we must put the fact that Jesus himself sometimes got angry. Mark (3.5) says flatly that when carping sabbatarians objected to the healing of the man with the withered hand, "Jesus looked around at them with anger."

The New Testament writers themselves seem uneasy about this. Matthew and Luke also report the incident, but neither of them records the anger. Luke says simply that "he looked around on them all" (Luke 6.10). Matthew omits all reference to this devastating look. It appears as if these two Evangelists considered that, even if it were true that Jesus was angry, it ought to be suppressed. Similarly, when officious disciples repulsed mothers eager to bring their children to the Master, Mark relates that "when Jesus saw it he was indignant" (10.14). Matthew and Luke again report the incident but omit all mention of Jesus' indignation.

Thomas Fuller, the seventeenth-century English clergyman and historian, says that "Anger is one of the sinews of the soul; he that wants it hath a maimed mind." Our moral difficulty with the emotion of anger is evident from this situation, that Matthew and Luke did not want to picture Jesus as ever having been angry, and tone down or omit Mark's vigorous words on that score. The tendency of the church, however, has been to make it easier for us to be angry, and Matthew (5.22) has been amended so as to make clear provision for what we call righteous indignation.

Perhaps Paul speaks for us here the clarifying word: "Be angry," he says (Eph. 4.26), "but do not sin." The cleansing of the Temple is an illustration of how Jesus became angry but did not sin. The Stoics forbade men to become angry at all. On that principle, Jesus would have said: "It is unfortunate that merchandising in the Temple precincts interferes with true religion, but after all these are good men and no doubt mean well; they are just mistaken." Reasoning thus, he might have been able to win friends and influence people sufficiently to have escaped the cross. In that case, of course, we never should have heard of him.

The fact is that he was not indifferent to this evil and did not seek to explain it away. The cleansing of the Temple was the act of an angry man but not of a sinful man. The story contains some hints about when to be angry and how to be angry without sinning. In the first place, the cleansing of the Temple was not carried out on the impulse of the moment: It was premeditated. Premeditated crimes the law considers more heinous than those done on the spur of the moment, under the impulse of some sudden and overpowering emotion. The thing is worse when a man deliberately plans to do it. So Jesus' act here gains in solemnity when we remember that the cleansing was not carried out when the defilement first came to his attention.

That is a very significant thing which Mark says of our Lord's actions following the triumphal entry: "when he had looked round at everything, as it was already late, he went out to Bethany" (11.11). It was not until later in the week that he carried out the cleansing. That is to say, before he acted on this impulse he slept over it. He saw what was wrong, but did not fly off into a rage. He took the thing home for prayer and meditation. It was only later, when duty had become clear, that he acted. His anger is not hot anger but cold anger.

Again, such violence as Jesus used was directed not upon the men but only upon the animals. That is something we are apt to miss in a careless reading of the story. The whip which he made was a "bunch of rushes," such as would be used for bedding the cattle—it is a pretty far cry from a bundle of straw to an atomic bomb. It appears that it was the sheep and cattle upon which Jesus used this little whip. It was not a show of violence sufficient to intimidate the men. Why then did they not resist? Jerome says: "a certain fiery and starry light shone from His eyes and the majesty of Godhead gleamed in His face."

Goodness has an ally in the breast of every man, and it was conscience that made cowards out of the cattle dealers.

It was that, rather than any show of physical force on our Lord's part that caused them to beat a hasty retreat. Our Lord's anger was deliberate and not impulsive; its effective force was moral and not physical. The Gospel tradition reveals, in spite of the reluctance of some of the reporters, that Jesus was angry on more than one occasion. It is important to consider the things which made Him angry.

In the first place, He seems to have been angry at anything which destroyed or injured the lives of persons, anything which interfered with the free play of personality. There was a time when the disciples felt insulted; they had not received the kind of welcome to which they felt entitled, and they said: "Lord, do you want us to bid fire come down from heaven and consume them?" But Jesus "turned and rebuked them . . . the Son of man came not to destroy men's lives but to save them" (Luke 9.54f). The disciples were angry at personal insult. Jesus never was, and rebuked them for being. Pre-eminently did Jesus become angry at those who would thwart or distort the unfolding life of childhood: "whoever causes one of these little ones who believe in me to sin, it would be better for him to have a great millstone fastened round his neck and to be drowned in the depth of the sea" (Mt. 18.6).

Another thing that made Jesus angry was that stupid conventionalism which assumes that institutions are more important than people. In his time the day of rest had become a fetish, and it was more important not to do any work on it than it was to bring health and healing to man whose infirmity prevented him from doing useful work at any time. That kind of formal, external, legalistic religion Jesus labeled hypocrisy. To Pharisees who thought that creeds and ceremonial were more important than people he said things we should not want our children to repeat. He called them snakes and whited sepulchres and blind fools.

Undoubtedly whoever is angry is in danger, but anger can be managed. Our difficulty is that we are usually angry at the wrong things and at the wrong times. George Matheson, the hymn writer, wrote in his journal: "Looking back over my life I feel there were times when I would have done well to be angry, but I fear I have mistaken the times." J. B. Priestley said of H. G. Wells that "When he was angry, it was because he knew ... that life need not be a sordid, greedy scramble." Let us be sure that our wrath is directed at the right things. Then we may know what it is to "Be angry, and not sin." He who has mastered anger can walk through life much more serenely.

18. Look Carefully How You Walk

James Hocking said on his 100th birthday, "I feel better at 100 than I did at 95." A former champion at distance walking, Hocking still takes a daily stroll. Noting that his grandson was engaged in automobile racing, he added: "I suppose the next thing will be jet planes." For many Americans now, "walk" is something one does only when the downtown traffic signal tells him to. These flashing neon signs, however, can be confusing. Visiting Washington, D. C., for the first time, a lady deliberately crossed the street when the sign said, "Don't walk." Arrested for her misdemeanor, she explained to the judge that she thought "Don't walk" was an advertisement urging people to ride the buses. Confusion in this respect reaches its ultimate in a southern city where at one complicated intersection the sign reads: "Walk to Here on Don't Walk."

The Scripture regularly speaks of our whole life as if it were a walk. There are not less than four hundred references in our English Bible to the word "walk"; few words have so many entries in a concordance. This usage appears throughout the Bible. Making their escape from Egypt, the Hebrews had no airlift. Instead, "the people of Israel walked on dry ground through the sea" (Ex. 14.29). After that, "the people of Israel walked forty years in the wilderness" (Josh. 5.6). When they crossed over Jordan, too, "the soles of the priests' feet were lifted up on dry ground" (Josh 4.18). During all this time, when the people were faithful to the nation's God they were said to "walk in his ways" (Deut. 28.9). When they forgot who it was that saved them, they were said to "go after other gods" (Deut. 8.19).

As historians report on the rule of Israel's kings, they tell us how each man walked. "Solomon loved the LORD, walking in the statutes of David his father" (1 Kings 3.3). Abijam, on the other hand, "walked in all the sins which his father did before him" (1 Kings 15.3). Jehoram "walked in the ways of the kings of Israel, as the house of Ahab had done" (2 Kings 8.18).

In the Psalms the upright man is one "who walks not in the counsel of the wicked" (Psalm 1.1); "who walk(s) in the law of the LORD" (Psalm 119.1).

"No good thing does the LORD withhold
from those who walk uprightly" (Psalm 84.11).

Sages, too, praised the man who knew how to walk aright:

"He who walks in integrity walks securely" (Prov. 10.9).

"He who trusts in his own mind is a fool:
but he who walks in wisdom will be delivered (Prov. 28.26).

When Harold Macmillan succeeded Anthony Eden as British Prime Minister, Henry Brooke became Minister of

Housing. Brooke is a grandson of the Rev. Stopford Brooke, an Anglican clergyman of poetic bent, whose hymns include a childhood favorite beginning,

"It fell upon a summer day,
When Jesus walked in Galilee."

The Gospels do represent the ministry of Jesus as a constant itineration, on foot. "As he walked by the Sea of Galilee, he saw two brothers" (Mt. 4.18). John the Baptizer "looked at Jesus as he walked, and said 'Behold the Lamb of God!'" (John 1.36). In Jerusalem, Jesus "was walking in the temple" (John 10.23). He "who follows me," said he (John 8.12), "will not walk in darkness."

It is not surprising, then, to find the apostles giving us all sorts of advice about how we ought to walk. Christ died for us, says Paul (Romans 6.4), that "we might walk in newness of life"; "we walk by faith, not by sight" (2 Cor. 5.7); "walk in love" (Eph. 5.2). Our concern for fellow travelers is the test of discipleship: "If your brother is being injured by what you eat, you are no longer walking in love" (Rom. 14.15). "If we say we have fellowship with him while we walk in darkness, we lie" (I John 1:6); "he who says he abides in him (i.e. Christ) ought to walk in the same way in which he walked" (I John 2.6).

Walking is many things: exercise, recreation, meditation, and reflection. As exercise it involves no preparation—not even a change of clothes. To work on the parallel bars, you must put on a gym suit. To play tennis, you must don rubber-soled shoes without heels. To play golf or go swimming, you must travel to the park or club. But no time need be lost in getting ready for a walk. Games must be played on a pre-scribed field—diamond, court, or fairway. On a walk one need never follow the same course twice. There is always a change of faces, a change of scenery, a change of incidents to witness. Games depend upon daylight and good weather, but a walk is fun any time.

Even when the weather is bad, it is never (as John Kiernan once observed) as bad as it looks through the window. Kagawa, the great Japanese Christian, says: "I am passionately fond of the pouring rain ... The rain is my comrade. Nothing equals the pleasure of walking, umbrellaless and free through the pelting, pouring rain." Charles Lamb knew a walk could be fun any hour of the twenty-four. "Is any nightwalk comparable," he asks, "to a walk from St. Paul's to Charing Cross, for lighting and paving, crowds going and coming without respite, the rattle of coaches, and the cheerfulness of shops." It was Lamb, too, who was sure that a walk ought to be begun with a religious ceremonial. He does not understand why grace should be said only at mealtimes. "I am disposed to say grace upon twenty other occasions," he writes. "I want a form for setting out upon a pleasant walk, for a moonlight ramble, for a friendly meeting, or a solved problem."

It is no accident that the author of the *Essays of Elia* thought simultaneously of a pleasant walk and a solved problem. A Latin proverb has it *solvitur ambulando*. This is interpreted to mean, "difficulties will disappear as the matter proceeds." The literal meaning is, "it is solved by walking"—the solution to his perplexity has come to many a man while he strolled. A character in the popular radio program, "Halls of Ivy," once introduced the idea that walking and thinking are two things that go together, and that the reason people now seem to think so little is that they walk so little.

The school of philosophers called "Peripatetics" got its name from the Greek word meaning "walk about." It is this word which often occurs in the New Testament. "Walk" is used of conduct and manner of life. This figure of speech comes to us from an age in which dignitaries might have chariots, but the common people had no mechanical means of transportation. Nevertheless there are values here which an age of speedy locomotion needs to relearn. A science fiction writer penned a story called "The Pedestrian." A man goes out for a walk and a robot police car eases up beside him, demanding to know why he is walking. "To breathe some air," he answers. The robot says: "But you've got an air conditioner." "I wanted to see things," the man says. "But you've got a television set," the robot says—and hurries the pedestrian off to an insane asylum.

Walking is sound therapy for many of the things that trouble. A druggist said that a half hour's brisk walk at bedtime would do more to assure a good night's rest than all the sleeping pills in his store. President Eisenhower urged young Americans to go in for bicycling in order to improve the Nation's physical stamina. The Dutch, who have only one automobile for every forty citizens, do more bicycling than the people of other lands. They have a longer life-span, too, than the people of any other country. Many of the values of bicycling can be had by walking. Dr. Stanley Rivlin, director of the London Varicose Clinic, told the American College of Angiology (specialists in diseases of the heart and blood vessels) that he advised his patients, "walk away your leg ulcers." He reported that in his treatment of ulcerated legs, walking had been successful in effecting a cure in 95 per cent of the cases. "The trouble is," he added, "you virtually have to brain-wash the patients to get them to walk."

In the vivid language of the Old Testament, God Himself is thought of as a foot passenger. Genesis (3.8) relates that our first parents "heard the sound of the LORD God walking in the garden in the cool of the day." In Leviticus (26.12) God says: "And I will walk among you, and will be your God, and you shall be my people." In the book of Deuteronomy, cleanliness in our earthly surroundings is enjoined because God walks among us. Moses says to the people (Deut. 23.14): "Because the LORD your God walks in the midst of your camp ... therefore your camp must be holy." In one of the apocryphal books, the returning exiles are promised that "God Himself will walk at the head of the caravan, leading them with joy." The last book in the Bible tells us of God's glory: "By its light shall the nations walk" (Rev. 21.24). Describing the death of one Old Testament worthy, Genesis (5.24) speaks as if he and God had simply gone out for a walk together. "Enoch walked with God; and he was not, for God took him." By speaking of life as a walk on which we could have the Divine companionship, the Scripture means to tell us that the everyday cares of life are God's concern, and our daily duty can be performed in His company.

A quarter of a century ago the editorial page of *The New York Times* made almost daily reference to the Bible. One of the editors was Dr. John H. Finley, who grew up on a farm in Illinois. Following the furrows, he kept a Bible strapped to the plow handle and said that Amos and Isaiah and Jeremiah and other Biblical characters were more real to him than the boys on the next farm. When he moved to the city, Dr. Finley retained his farm habits. On week ends he often walked from New York to Princeton, and every year on his birthday walked around Manhattan Island. His advice to the young was: "Read a book, make a friend, take a walk." When he died the minister read Isaiah (40.31):

> "They who wait for the Lord
>> shall renew their strength,
>> they shall mount up with wings like eagles,
>> they shall run and not be weary,
>>> they shall walk and not faint."

They who can walk in this way will be able also to labor with less fatigue.

19. The Sacrament of Labor

Seeking to encourage Europeans to come to America, Benjamin Franklin wrote that God is a mechanic who "is respected and admired more for the variety, ingenuity, and utility of his handiworks, than for the antiquity of his family." This conception of Deity no doubt helped to determine the nature of the society which developed on this continent. Settlers had come from lands where only certain classes worked, but here each man was expected to make his fair contribution with hand and brain. An early Virginia law decreed that any idler was to be assigned by the magistrate to some one who should make him work for wages "till he shewe apparent signes of amendment." Writing of seventeenth-century Maryland, a historian says: "the son works as well as the servant, so that before they eat their bread they are commonly taught how to earn it."

Reference to God as a mechanic is not the language ordinarily used about Deity, but it does not do violence to the Genesis story of creation where God is Himself represented as taking delight in "the variety, ingenuity, and utility of his handiworks." Following the account of each day's creative activity, the inspired writer tells us that "God saw that it was good" (Genesis 1.10, 12, 18, 21, 25). Finally looking back upon His whole week's work, "God saw everything that he had made, and behold, it was very good" (Genesis 1.31). One of the books of the Apocrypha suggests that God's joy in creation was reflected in the objects of his handiwork. Baruch (3.34) says of the stars, "they shone with gladness for him who made them."

113

The Genesis story fondly traces, too, the beginnings of the several occupations among men. "Abel was a keeper of sheep, and Cain a tiller of the ground" (Gen. 4.2). Nimrod is a term we still apply to any one skilled as a huntsman. Genesis (10.8f) tells of the original Nimrod: "he was the first on earth to be a mighty man. He was a mighty hunter before the Lord." Jabal "was the father of those who dwell in tents and have cattle. His brother's name was Jubal; he was the father of all those who play the lyre and pipe" (Gen. 4:20f). Tubal-cain "was the forger of all instruments of bronze and iron" (Gen. 4.22). Thus the Hebrews fondly traced the ancestry of our humankind. Our forebears were all workmen—not a gentleman in the lot!

The Old Testament gives two reasons for the sabbath rest, both of them associated with toil. Exodus (20.11) seems to speak as if God the workman was weary at the end of six days' toil and needed a day off: "in six days the LORD made heaven and earth, the sea, and all that is in them, and rested the seventh day; therefore the LORD blessed the sabbath day and hallowed it." In Deuteronomy, however, the Hebrews are reminded that in Egypt they had to work hard, and this is the reason they must now give everybody a day off: "You shall remember that you were a servant in the land of Egypt" (Deut. 5.15).

In preparation for worship in the wilderness, everybody worked. God commanded Moses to "speak to all who have ability, whom I have endowed with an able mind" (Ex. 28.3; cf. 31.6). Each man toiled according to his own skills. Some made such "practical" things as "shovels and basins and forks and fire pans" (Ex. 27.3). Others perfected priestly garments which should be "for glory and for beauty" (Ex. 28.2, 40). It is an interesting commentary upon that ancient society that the women also worked: "all women who had ability spun with their hands" (Ex. 35.25), some working on linen, others on goats' hair.

The book of Ecclesiastes is filled with cynicism. Its author finds most things on earth disappointing. Friends cannot always be counted on: "One man among a thousand I found," he says (Eccles. 7.28), "but a woman among all these I have not found." Increase in this world's goods does not really bring security: "He who loves money will not be satisfied with money" (Eccles. 5.10). We are accustomed to teach the young that the pursuit of education is better than the pursuit of wealth, yet this author is sure that the mere accumulation of facts is of itself no better than collecting matchbox covers, postage stamps or golden coins:

> "For in much wisdom is much vexation,
>   and he who increases knowledge increases sorrow"
>   (Eccles. 1.18).

Most of man's pursuits this writer dismisses as "a striving after wind." The wisdom literature is replete with similes for describing man's attempt to do what he ought not:

> "He who meddles in a quarrel not his own
>   is like one who takes a passing dog by the ears"
>   (Prov. 26.17).

> "A continual dripping on a rainy day
>   and a contentious woman are alike;
>   to restrain her is to restrain the wind
>   or to grasp oil in his right hand"
>   (Prov. 27.15, 16).

> "Who has gathered the wind in his fists?"
>   (Prov. 30.4).

Most of the things that men desire the gentle cynic considers equally futile. In the King James Version they are described as "a vexation of spirit." In the Biblical languages, as in many other tongues, the same word is used for wind, breath, spirit. It is this play on words which lends point to one of our Lord's utterances, recorded in John (3.8): Jesus says to Nicodemus: "The wind blows where it wills, and you hear the sound of it, but you do not know whence it comes or whither it goes, so it is with every one who is born of the Spirit." So in the Old Testament, the same Hebrew word may be translated either wind or spirit. In the Ecclesiastes references the King James translators chose the latter. They regard the search after knowledge (1.17), the rewards of toil (2.11), the acquisition of an estate (2.23), envy of one's neighbor (4.4), the sovereignty exercised by a king (4.16), indeed all the experiences of life (2.17) as "a vexation of spirit."

The King James Version is not consistent with itself at this point. Where similar language is employed in Hosea (12.1), that translation reads: "Ephraim feedeth on wind, and followeth after the east wind." The REVISED STANDARD VERSION gives this vivid rendering also in Ecclesiastes. Instead of "a vexation of spirit" we have, in all the above references, "a striving after wind." For the author of Ecclesiastes, most of the things we consider important are quickly "gone with the wind." Nor is his cynicism about matters on the earth relieved by any hope of immortality. For him, there is nothing eternal to which man may look forward: "He who is joined with all the living has hope, for a living dog is better than a dead lion" (Eccles. 9.4).

He is particularly cynical about the heaping up of goods in which so many suppose they will find security. Since a man cannot take it with him, the money he heaped together may be left either to "a man who did not toil for it" (Eccles. 2.21) or, if he has no heir, to some one outside the family altogether, and "a stranger enjoys" it (Eccles. 6.2). While making it clear that the accumulated rewards of toil can themselves be no guarantee of happiness, the one thing concerning which the author appears to have no cynicism is work itself and the satisfactions that come from forgetting oneself in honest toil! He believes that for every man, "to accept his lot and find enjoyment in his toil—this is the gift of God" (Eccles. 5.19); "it is God's gift to man that every one should eat and drink and take pleasure in all his toil" (Eccles. 3.13).

Now this is a very far cry from "the gift of God" as it is envisioned in the New Testament. There our Lord himself is spoken of as "God's inexpressible gift" (2 Cor. 9.15). Paul is so concerned to emphasize the primacy of God's grace that he regards even the ability to accept this gift as itself a gift: "by grace you have been saved through faith; and this is not your own doing, it is the gift of God" (Eph. 2.8). Nevertheless the author of Ecclesiastes is not out of harmony with the rest of the Scripture when he refers to opportunity for honest toil as God's gift to our race.

The church celebrates Pentecost as the day God's Spirit came upon man in its fulness. The first Biblical character, however, to have been filled with the Spirit of God was a workman. Bezaleel was in charge of wood, metal, and stone work for the tabernacle. In Exodus (31.3-5) God says: "I have filled him with the Spirit of God, with ability and intelligence, with knowledge and all craftsmanship, to devise artistic designs, to work in gold, silver, and bronze, in cutting stones for setting, and in carving wood, for work in every craft."

There was a saying among the rabbis that a father who did not teach his son a trade was as guilty as if he had taught him robbery. So it came about that Christianity's first and greatest missionary was an artisan. Paul the tentmaker was proud that he accepted no gifts from the Thessalonians. "For you yourselves know," he writes (2 Thess. 3.7f), "how you ought to imitate us; we were not idle when we were with you, we did not eat any one's bread without paying, but with toil and labor we worked night and day, that we might not burden any of you." From beginning to end, the healthy-minded men and women of the Bible were not afraid to work.

The Gospels do not begin to tell us all that Jesus said or did. As if to leave the matter open for future discovery, the Gospel according to John concludes (21.25): "But there are also many other things which Jesus did: were every one of them to be written, I suppose that the world itself could not contain the books that would be written." Archaeologists' "delving spades" have set free some of the sayings of Jesus buried for centuries in Egyptian sands. In the 1890's Grenfell and Hunt found some papyrus leaves which contained sayings of Jesus not found in the canonical gospels. These sayings appear to have been collected without reference to the incidents which called them forth.

One of these sayings Henry Van Dyke, in his poem "A Lost Word of Jesus," has called "the sacrament of labor." It suggests that God's presence is to be found wherever men toil in honor and sincerity. It also puts in a different light the uneasiness which the author of Ecclesiastes felt with regard to certain types of manual labor:

> "He who quarries stones is hurt by them;
> and he who splits logs is endangered by them"
>
> (Eccles. 10.9).

Perhaps with specific reference to that, Jesus has given what Van Dyke calls "Gospel for the heavy-laden, answer to the labourer's cry." The new-found saying is this: "Raise the stone and you will find me; cleave the wood, and there am I." This gives one a new appreciation of the realm of nature.

20. The Trees Clap Their Hands

When a Yale professor declared in *Life* magazine that Sunday school is "the most wasted hour of the week," religious educators were quick to point out that this was criticism within a "narrow framework." The twentieth-century church, they said, does not depend upon a few hurried moments on Sunday morning for imparting the faith to the younger generation. "Tremendous learnings," as one of them put it, flow from other activities such as summer camps and conferences. A feature of the latter often is worship out-of-doors. One conference held worship early in the morning, with the preacher in a little boat and the congregation along the shore. Reminiscent of what took place in our Lord's time, this was called a "Galilean service."

Other groups held "tryst" at evening. At a New England camp the vesper site was a point of land jutting out into the lake. Worship was held at sunset, while the sun dropped behind the western horizon on the other side of the lake. One leader refused to attend, saying that all who did so were sun worshipers. Denying that God could be found in nature, he alleged that his young charges were not Christians but druids. A theological movement in recent years has tended to deny that God was to be found in nature—or at least that any saving knowledge of God was to be found there.

Difficulty at this point arises because we bring to the Scripture thought-forms out of the Western world. We make a distinction between nature and spirit, between natural religion and revealed religion. This is a distinction which the Bible does not make. God was everywhere and immediately present. A German poet says: "If thou wouldst attain to thy highest,

119

go look upon a flower, and what that does unconsciously do thou consciously." In the Scripture all the graces and virtues of life are symbolized by the wonders of forest and field and mountain. A lonely Japanese boy thought himself "doomed to a life-horizon that is common and colorless." Missionaries came into his life and told him of a God who cares. One of them took him out under the open sky, turned his tear-stained face toward the sun, and said: "Look at the sky, look at the sun, let your tears evaporate and then we will laugh."

The miracle had been wrought. The lad next began to read the Gospel: "Consider the lilies of the field, how they grow, they neither toil nor spin; yet I tell you, even Solomon in all his glory was not arrayed like one of these. But if God so clothes the grass of the field, which today is alive and to-morrow is thrown into the oven, will he not much more clothe you, O men of little faith?" (Mt. 6.28-30). The lad read and re-read the passage. He committed it to memory. Then he memorized the whole chapter. The fountains of the great deep were broken up in a poignant cry: "O God, make me like Christ." It was through this experience that Toyo-hiko Kagawa was born anew and began a life dedicated to the service of those for whom the world held no beauty.

C. F. Andrews was a missionary to India so devoted to the people among whom he lived that they insisted his initials really stood for Christ's Friendly Apostle. In his autobiography, which he calls *What I Owe to Christ,* Andrews recalls a critical period in his childhood. "For long month's together," he says, "my spirit had been hovering between life and death and I had almost lost the desire to live. Then one morning, when I opened my eyes, I noticed a flower by my bedside which my mother had put there while I was asleep, hoping that it would attract my attention when I awoke. It so happened that the sight of that flower proved the turning point in the struggle that had been going on within me, drawing me back to life, for its beauty touched me with a rare joy. It brought with it the desire to live, when life itself was hanging by a thread. My mother noticed in a moment the change which had come over me, after I had opened my eyes and welcomed the beauty of the flower."

It was not of course the flower alone that had such healing power. It was all that the flower symbolized, not only of God's delight in beauty but of his mother's tender thoughtfulness toward him: "It was her loving care that had placed it there, and it was in truth her constant prayer that had restored me. From that day my recovery went steadily forward and keen pleasure in life revived."

The Scripture represents the forest as making visible manifestation of its joy in God's presence:

> "Let the field exult, and everything in it!
> Then shall all the trees of the wood sing for joy
> before the LORD" (Psalm 96.12f).

In joyous moments of praise men involuntarily clap their hands. The prophet imagines the waving of the branches of the trees to have a similar significance:

> "The mountains and the hills before you
> shall break forth into singing,
> and all the trees of the field shall clap their
> hands" (Is. 55.12).

Referring to William Cullen Bryant's "Forest Hymn," Edgar Allan Poe wrote of the lines "of whose great rhythmical beauty it is scarcely possible to speak too highly." The poem begins:

> "The groves were God's first temples."

It is no accident that Gothic architecture has pointed arches sustained by "venerable columns." This was man's attempt to imitate the worshipful forms he found in the forest.

Bryant's hymn goes on to offer prayer:

> "Thou fill'st
>   The solitude. Thou art in the soft winds
>   That run along the summit of these trees
>   In music."

The story is told of a monk who went for a walk in the woods, heard a bird break into song, decided to stop and listen for a trill or two. Upon his return to the convent gate he found himself a stranger. He had been gone for fifty years, and only one of his old comrades survived to recognize him. Other lore, too, gathers around the forest. A Lithuanian immigrant recalls how in childhood he had asked his mother to explain the noises that were to be heard coming from the heart of the forest after sundown. She said they were the songs of joy uttered by departed animals that had lived freely. The heart of the forest was their heaven. "After I learned that story," says Louis Adamic, "the heart of the forest and all natural fastnesses were always holy places to me."

Woodsmen assure us that every color tint to which a tree has been exposed during its lifetime glows in the fire when that tree is burned. Look into the coals and embers of the fireplace and there you can find "the pinks and violet of dawn, the blueness of the sky, the burning brightness of the noonday sun, the angry black of a thunder-cloud, the crimson of the sunset, the silver radiance of the moonlight, the brilliant transparency of the stars." It was thoughts such as these which inspired John Oxenham's lines:

> "Kneel always when you light a fire!
> Kneel reverently, and thankful be
> For God's unfailing charity."

An American naturalist, Edwin Way Teale, wrote a book entitled *North with the Spring*. Beginning in the Florida Everglades in February, he and his wife followed spring northward until they reached the Vermont-Canadian border in June. Dogwood was in bloom all the way. The observers report that in the eastern part of the United States spring moves northward at an average rate of 15 miles a day. It moves up a mountain one hundred feet a day. The Irish poet and dramatist, John Millington Synge, tells us that the one thing he dreaded about death, the only thing that really made him sad, was "that while he lay there cloistered the seasons would come and go and he would know nothing of it at all."

The prophet Jeremiah relates how God spoke to him in the spring: "the word of the LORD came to me, saying, 'Jeremiah, what do you see?' and I said, 'I see a rod of almond.' Then the LORD said to me, 'you have seen well, for I am watching over my word to perform it'" (Jer. 1.11f). The point here rests upon a play on words found in the original but difficult to carry over into English. Footnotes in the REVISED STANDARD VERSION explain that the word translated "rod of almond" is in the Hebrew *SHAQED:* the word rendered "watching" is *SHOQED*. What Jeremiah saw was an almond-bough, with bright pink blossoms and pale green leaves. This token of an early spring, rising out of the dreariness of winter, was to him evidence that God was still at work in the world. The prophet was very young when he learned this lesson, and no prophet's work is more replete with imagery drawn from the natural world than the book which Jeremiah wrote.

It is related of St. Francis of Assisi that the warmth and brilliance of the sunshine summoned him back to life after a severe illness. Fever and pain caused him for weeks to toss in delirium. It was the sun shining through his window which first roused him from his semiconscious state. During his recuperation his days were measured by the coming and going of the sun. Not only did it help him to move his stiffened limbs, but the wish to see it arise in the morning and to keep it in sight as long as possible in the evening led him to sit up in bed and so "overcome the heavy torpor of his ailing body." St. Francis' Canticle of the Sun is regarded by many as the finest expression of religious feeling that has come down to us from the middle ages. It reads in part:

> "Praised be my Lord God, with all His creatures,
>   and especially our brother the Sun, who
>   brings us the day and who brings us the light:
>   fair is he, and he shines with a very great splendor.
> O Lord, he signifies us to thee!"

The Scripture represents the sun as symbolizing the splendor of God which also sympathizes with the moods of man. In the heavens, says the Psalmist (19.04f) God

> "has set a tent for the sun,
>   which comes forth like a bridegroom leaving his
>   chamber   ,
>   and like a strong man runs its course with joy."

One of the oldest portions of the Bible is a song which Joshua sang when God's ancient people needed more time in which to complete a victory in the battle for the Land of Promise:

> "Sun, stand thou still at Gibeon,
>   and thou Moon in the valley of Aijalon"
>   (Josh. 10.12).

Our book of Joshua quotes a now lost work, called the Book of Jashar, to the effect that "The sun stayed in the midst of heaven, and did not hasten to go down for about a whole day" (Josh. 10.13). On the other hand, when our Lord died the sun could not bear to look upon the sight, and "there was darkness over the whole land until the ninth hour" (Mark 15.33).

There are contemporary theologians who assure us that nature cannot possibly have any redemptive or healing power, but, as William James reminds us, " a large acquaintance with particulars often makes us wiser than the possession of abstract formulas." In scientific experiments one proven instance is held to have established the case. If Kagawa and C. F. Andrews and St. Francis of Assisi were won to life and health through the Gospel proclaimed in nature, then it is time to quit saying that nature has no healing power.

This matter is set in true perspective in Paul's letter to the Romans where he insists that pagans are "men who by wickedness suppress the truth. For what can be known about God is plain to them, because God has shown it to them. Ever since the creation of the world his invisible nature, namely, his eternal power and deity, has been clearly perceived in the things that have been made. So they are without excuse" (Romans 1:18-20). The Gospel goes far beyond this, though, in giving us an outline of what we are privileged to believe.

21. Peace in Believing

The twentieth century has been poor in biographies of great religious leaders. What has it to offer in comparison with the life-stories of Jonathan Edwards, Alexander Whyte, Phillips Brooks? The lack has been in some measure made up by recent studies of men like Robert E. Speer, Henry Sloane Coffin, and Harry Emerson Fosdick. Walter Russell Bowie set out to write a biographical study of Henry Sloane Coffin, but found that Dr. Coffin could hardly be captured by the pen of a friend, and that he ought to be allowed to speak for himself. He therefore made a collection of Dr. Coffin's prayers, and excerpts from his sermons. This he published under the title, *Joy in Believing*. That is a Scriptural phrase, but only part of the phrase. Paul hopes that his friends in Rome may have "joy and peace in believing" (Rom. 15.13).

Dr. Coffin did have joy in believing. Walter Pater in *Marius the Epicurean*, described the spirit of the new Christian society as it appeared to a pagan of that age. He spoke of its demand for sacrifice and went on to say that "it issued in a certain debonair grace, and a certain mystic attractiveness and courtesy, which made Marius doubt whether that famed Greek blitheness or gaiety or grace in the handling of life had been, after all, an unrivaled success." Thus Christianity beat the Greeks at their own game, and this has been nowhere more apparent than in the life of Henry Sloane Coffin. Born to privilege, he scorned a life of ease and took upon himself the burden of the slum-folk in New York. The social standing and prestige which were his through family connections, he used to compel the fashionable people of the Madison Avenue Presbyterian Church to accept into their fellowship those who had formerly worshiped at a mission chapel in Yorkville. When one great lady complained that "these people smelled," Dr. Coffin asked whether she hadn't the grace to recognize the odor of sanctity.

Whether informally with a group of friends or in the tenseness of ecclesiastical debate, whether surrounded by admiring young men or facing die-hard opponents, Dr. Coffin always exhibited the ready wit and gracious manner of one whose life was fed from the deepest springs of Christian Joy. When many of his contemporaries were turning to gloomy views of life and human nature, he maintained the serenity of one who had communed with the Eternal. Dr. Coffin's joy was bound up with what Dr. Coffin believed. As his friend and colleague, Dr. Bowie, puts it: "Only in the strength of that could he have accomplished his manifold ministry in a generation when the faith of many wavered before the hard facts of the Twentieth Century world. Henry Coffin never evaded those facts; but in his own experience he knew a mightier Fact."

If ever we are to have peace, it must come through believing. Only, we must believe the right things! If we are to have peace in believing, then, our beliefs must correspond with reality. We must believe, not in fancies, but in fact. The prophet Jeremiah lived at a time when gross injustices were rife in the land, but there were those who thought they could gloss over evil times by saying everything would be all right. Priests and false prophets alike joined in a conspiracy to conceal the true nature of the situation. The faithful prophet will have none of this, but cries out:

> "They have healed the wound of my people lightly,
>   saying, 'Peace, peace,'
>   when there is no peace" (Jer. 6.14).

Voodoo is a form of religion brought to the western world by captives from Africa. One of its features is the snake dance, in which torpid reptiles are set down uncovered in the midst of a circle, round which the worshipers dance. Should a snake try to escape and, being stepped on, bite a naked foot, an antidote is kept in readiness. One wonders whether this is the origin of snake-handling as practiced by cults in the south. Such groups speak much of "faith," and say that one will not be harmed by a snake if only he has faith enough. It is fantastic, however, to believe that snakes will not bite. That is the nature of snakes, and no real peace can come to any one who falsifies that. The number of people bitten in recent years and the constant threat posed by snake-handling have led the legislatures of several southern states to outlaw the practice.

There can be no real peace for any one who builds his home on the side of a live volcano in the belief that it may not erupt. It is the nature of a volcano to erupt. There can be no real peace for any one who goes to sea in a boat that is too frail, in the belief that no storm will arise. It is the nature of wind and wave to toss our boats around. There is no peace in believing that the wave will abandon its crushing power merely because our bark is weak, and that the wind will cease merely because it is tearing our sails to pieces.

> "Storms will not curb their pride
>   The just man not to entomb,
>   Nor lightnings go aside
>   To give his virtues room,
> Nor is that wind less rough that blows a good man's barge."

There is no peace in believing that good people will never have to suffer. Jesus told the story of the two men, each of whom built a house. One built on sand; "and the rain fell, and the floods came, and the wind blew and beat against that house, and it fell" (Mt. 7.27). The other built upon rock. Did that mean that he escaped the buffeting of the storm? By no means. His house was subjected to exactly the same lashings by the forces of nature: "the rain fell, and the floods came, and the winds blew and beat upon that house" (Mt. 7.25). The reason it did not fall was, not that it escaped either flood or storm, but rather that its owner was right in believing that a house with a good foundation could stand.

There is no peace in believing that all suffering is punishment for sin. When the disciples saw "a man blind from his birth," they asked Jesus, "who sinned, this man or his parents, that he was born blind?" Jesus answered, "It was not that this man sinned, or his parents, but that the works of God might be made manifest in him" (John 9.1-3). Some suffering undoubtedly is caused by sin—our own or others'—but it is our Lord's teaching that this is not invariably the case. There is a mystery here beyond which we cannot probe.

Job's friends seek to bring him peace of mind by trying to convince him that any suffering he endures must be in punishment for sin. Respite, they say, will come only as he recognizes this and gives in. But Job knows this is not the case. He brushes aside their conventional consolations:

> "I desire to argue my case with God.
> As for you, you whitewash with lies;
>   worthless physicians are you all" (Job 13.4).

The real danger in false beliefs is more accurately described here than in the King James Version, where Job is represented as saying: "But ye are forgers of lies, ye are all physicians of no value." It was not that they had to scrape up or patch together a series of falsehoods. These are always ready to hand. What they intended was to use these to obscure the real truth of the situation. They were covering it with whitewash, and so proved themselves "plasterers of lies." The physician who deliberately obscures the nature of the disease will be powerless to heal.

There is no peace in believing that when we suffer God has turned his back upon us, nor that in affliction the Father's love has abandoned us. Hebrews (12.6) says:

> "For the Lord disciplines him whom he loves,
>   and chastises every son whom he receives."

The author admits that "For the moment all discipline seems painful rather than pleasant" (Heb. 12.11), but goes on to add: "later it yields the peaceful fruit of righteousness to those who have been trained by it." The King James Version here tells us that "afterward it yieldeth the peaceable fruit of righteousness unto them which are exercised thereby." To be exercised over something conveys to us the thought of being greatly wrought up or perturbed by it. The real significance here, however, is that appropriate response to suffering can discipline and strengthen character.

There is no peace in believing that we have sinned so greatly that we can never be forgiven. There is no peace in believing that our guilt is so great it can never be cleansed by God's grace. There is no peace in believing that, since God is just, He is bound to make us suffer the full consequences of our sin. The Scripture at this point uses a different argument from that which the logic of men would urge upon us. We read in I John (1.9): "If we confess our sins, he is faithful and just, and will forgive our sins and cleanse us from all unrighteousness." Our human reason would lead us to believe that, since God is just, He must punish our sins. But God's justice means that He cannot be untrue to His own nature. His nature is to forgive the penitent. If we make full confession and in repentance set out upon a new way of life, His justice requires that He forgive.

The Psalm (106.12) tells us of the children of Israel at one point in God's dealings with them:

"Then they believed his words;
they sang his praise."

The gratitude that comes from true believing can do wonders for us. The author of Psalm 27 (13) exclaimed:

"I believe that I shall see the goodness of the LORD
in the land of the living!"

Paul, too, was confident of this, and in a storm at sea he was sure of reaching his destination. With words such as these

he calmed his fellow passengers: "Take heart, men, for I
have faith in God that it will be exactly as I have been told"
(Acts 27.25). Here is the kind of belief which delivers from
hurry and anxiety. This the prophet knew long ago when
he wrote:

"He who believes will not be in haste" (Is. 28.16).

Concerning the God whom they trusted, two New Testament writers tell us: "he who believes in him will not be put
to shame" (Rom. 9.33; I Pet. 2.6). He who made and loves
us is concerned to save all there is of us. The medieval Church
seemed primarily concerned with saving souls. The Gospel
goes far beyond that.

22. Not Souls but Lives

A theological professor was accustomed to offer his beginning students the following multiple-choice question:

Jesus came to save:

     a. Men's lives.
     b. Souls from hell.
     c. People from their sins.
     d. Whatever is lost.

When asked which of these ideas best accorded with the
Bible, the men invariably chose b, and were shocked beyond
belief at being told that that is the only one which is not
Biblical. The Christmas message to Joseph was: "you shall
call his name Jesus, for he will save his people from their
sins" (Mt. 1.21). Some late manuscripts contain the saying
found in the King James Version at Luke (9.56): "the Son
of man is not come to destroy men's lives, but to save them."

At Luke (19.10) Jesus himself says: "the Son of man came to seek and to save the lost."

When the students went on to insist that Jesus must have come to save souls from hell because that was what they had been taught all their lives, the professor offered a thousand dollars (which he never would have been able to pay!) to any one who would show him a Biblical passage which said that Jesus had come to save souls from hell. No one ever claimed the reward. Because of widespread popular misunderstanding at this point, it behooves us to look carefully at the Scriptural use of the word "soul."

One meaning of the word "soul" is simply "human being" or "person." This usage is familiar to us in such phrases as poor soul, kind soul, dear soul; or in such mathematical descriptions as "ten thousand souls." Several times, in the King James Bible, the term "souls" has no other connotation than that. This is illustrated in Romans (13.1) which, in the King James, reads: "Let every soul be subject unto the higher powers." If souls were in subjection to the ruling authority of the civil government, this would seem to contradict our Lord's injunction, "Render therefore to Caesar the things that are Caesar's and to God the things that are God's" (Mt. 22.21). Surely the soul is one thing that belongs to God and not to Caesar!

The REVISED STANDARD VERSION is right therefore in rendering this: "Let every person be subject to the governing authorities." This usage is illustrated again in Acts (27.37), where Paul is describing the experience of shipwreck. "And we were in all in the ships, two hundred threescore and sixteen souls." This plainly is a passage which has no eschatological connotation, and "soul" is obviously a synonym for "person." RSV translates it: "We were in all two hundred and seventy-six persons in the ship."

Similarly in I Peter (3.20) which refers to Noah's ark

"wherein few, that is, eight souls were saved by water." The author uses this as suggesting baptism's efficacy. We are apt to find the analogy somewhat strained, since there were in Noah's time many more who were lost by water than the few who were saved by it. The point here, however, is that "souls" in that passage is just the equivalent of "persons" and this is recognized in practically all twentieth-century translations.

Again, in the description of the wonderful events which befell on the Day of Pentecost, Acts (2.41) in KJV says: "the same day there were added *unto them* three thousand souls." Because church statisticians are fond of supposing that what happens to souls can be indicated in annual ecclesiastical reports we have supposed that here is the conventional use of the term "souls." Three thousand souls saved in a single day —whereas we now have to preach 3,000 sermons to save a single soul! RSV is still under the spell of tradition at this point and has it read "there were added that day about 3,000 souls." Weymouth, however, makes it read: "and on that one day about 3,000 persons were added to them." Both Goodspeed and the Twentieth Century New Testament read "three thousand people."

Again, the word psyche sometimes simply means life, and it is so translated in the King James Version in Matthew (6.25). Jesus' injunction, "Take no thought for your life, what ye shall eat, or what ye shall drink" is, in the Greek, a command to have no anxious care about the psyche. The REVISED STANDARD translates the passage: "do not be anxious about your life, what you shall eat or what you shall drink." Not less than 40 times in the King James Version psyche is rendered "life."

In Luke (12.20) KJV has God say to the farmer who thought he could satisfy his soul with things: "*Thou* fool! this night thy soul shall be required of thee." Not even here

is it said that the man's soul is being sent to hell. It is said
that his soul "shall be required." "Required" in KJV is regularly used in its etymological sense of "call back." The man's
soul had been entrusted to him; he had done badly with it;
now it is being revoked. That is the interpretation placed
upon the passage by the KJV translators. It is not a faithful
rendering of the Greek, which says literally, "They are demanding your soul from you."

It is a vivid present tense—his soul is even now being
sought. Who the "they" are, however, is not specified. Some
would have it that the reference is to the death-bringing
angels mentioned in Job (33.22f). Others suppose that some
such word as "robbers" is to be supplied, as in Luke (10.30)
the robbers attacked the lone Samaritan on the Jericho road.
The robbers will get this man on the very night his wealth
has flowed in! Another suggestion is that a labor revolt was
developing, and that the passage really means "The peasants
whom you by your selfishness have now irritated beyond
endurance are now rising in mass against you."

Perhaps the plural is intended impersonally, much as we
say "they" are doing so and so, with reference to no particular persons. What we mean is that it is being done. The
REVISED STANDARD VERSION thus translates it: "your soul is
required of you," thus preserving, as the King James does
not, the correct tense, even if it does change a third person
plural active verb into a third person singular passive. In any
case, it is not said that the man's soul will tonight go down
to hell, but only that somebody, whether angels or robbers
or angry sharecroppers, is already knocking at the door,
demanding that it be given up.

What is it that the robbers can take from a man? Surely
not his soul—they can have no dominion over that. They can
do no more than take away his life, and the Twentieth Century New Testament renders the passage: "Fool! This very

night your life is being demanded." Weymouth's rendering is similar: "Foolish man, this night your life is demanded from you." It accords with this that we read in Matthew (2.20): "those who sought the child's life are dead." The minions of Herod were after precisely the same thing, the *psyche*, as those who lay in wait for the foolish farmer.

In other contexts the King James Version itself sometimes translates *psyche* by "life," as in Luke (9.24): "For whosoever will save his life shall lose it: but whosoever will lose his life for my sake, the same shall save it." Both occurrences of "life" in that passage translate "psyche." Similarly, at Revelation (12.11) the King James says: "And they overcame him by the blood of the Lamb and by the word of their testimony, and they loved not their lives unto the death." The word there translated "lives" is *psyche* in the plural. In each of the following passages, too, the King James renders *psyche* by "life": "Whosoever shall seek to save his life shall lose it; and whosoever shall lose his life shall preserve it" (Luke 17.33). "He that loveth his life shall lose it; and he that hateth his life in this world, shall keep it unto life eternal."

In Mark (8.35ff; and the parallel in Mt. 16.25f) the King James is curiously inconsistent. The word psyche, occurring four times in the passage, is twice translated "life" and twice translated "soul": "For whosoever will save his life shall lose it; but whosoever shall lose his life for my sake and the gospel's, the same shall save it. For what shall it profit a man, if he shall gain the whole world and lose his own soul? Or what shall a man give in exchange for his soul?" The REVISED STANDARD VERSION renders psyche the same way at each occurrence in the passage: "For whoever would save his life will lose it; and whoever loses his life for my sake and the gospel's will save it. For what does it profit a man, to gain the whole world and forfeit his life? For what can a man give in return for his life?"

In Luke (9.24f) there is a parallel passage in which psyche seems to be equated with the self: "For whoever would save his life will lose it; and whoever loses his life for my sake, he will save it. For what does it profit a man if he gains the whole world and loses or forfeits himself?"

At least twice in the REVISED STANDARD VERSION the word *psyche* is rendered mind: "The unbelieving Jews stirred up the Gentiles and poisoned their minds against the brethren" (Acts 14.2); "with one mind striving side by side for the faith of the gospel" (Phil. 1.27).

The *psyche* sometimes refers to the whole person. The farmer who forgot God thinks it is his *psyche* which can delight in the contemplation of his abundance. The psyche will not only feel a sense of security but it will relish the food and drink that go along with fine living: "I will say to my soul, Soul, you have ample goods laid up for many years; take your ease, eat, drink, be merry" (Luke 12.19). On the other hand, it is the soul which is able to enjoy the rest and peace that come from bearing our Lord's yoke: "Take my yoke upon you, and learn from me; for I am gentle and lowly in heart, and you will find rest for your souls" (Mt. 11.29).

Henry Drummond, a Scottish thinker who combined theology with an interest in the natural world, taught science at the Free Church College in Glasgow. He wrote *Natural Law in the Spiritual World,* lectured in America on "The Ascent of Man," and preached an often reprinted sermon, "The Greatest Thing in the World." D. L. Moody said of him, "He is a Christian who lives continuously in the 13th chapter of I Corinthians." Addressing young people in the universities of Britain and America, Drummond was fond of saying: "I ask you to become Christians not because you may die tonight but because you are going to live tomorrow. I come not to save your souls but to save your lives." In what does knowledge of salvation consist?

23. *Knowledge of Salvation*

Another multiple-choice question posed by the theological professor was this:

Salvation means

    a. Passengers' escape from shipwreck.
    b. Recovery of sick people from illness.
    c. Deliverance of souls from hell.

Beginning students invariably chose c. as the correct answer, and were unfailingly shocked to discover that the other two represent explicit Biblical ideas on the subject.

More than once in the New Testament, happy escape from a storm at sea is described as salvation. When the disciples' boat was about to be swamped by the waves and Jesus was asleep in the stern, "They went and woke him, saying, 'Save Lord, we are perishing'" (Mt. 8.25). Of Peter, trying to walk on the water, it is recorded (Mt. 14.30), "When he saw the wind, he was afraid, and beginning to sink he cried out, 'Lord save me.'" When frightened sailors were trying to escape from a storm-tossed boat in the Mediterranean, Paul, the one calm passenger on board, said: "Unless these men stay in the ship, you cannot be saved" (Acts 27.31).

Paul, who by this time seems to have taken charge of the vessel, said: "I urge you to take some food; it will give you strength" (Acts 27.34). The word here translated "strength" is the word (*soteria*) which, at many other places in the New Testament is translated "salvation." If we should insist on giving it this connotation here, we should have Paul demanding that the ship's company take a little food for the sake of their eternal salvation. Plainly "salvation" in all these instances simply means rescue from disaster at sea. At Philippians (1.19) Paul writes: "I know that through your prayers and the help of the Spirit of Jesus Christ this will turn out for my deliverance." Here is the same word, *soteria*. In this case it means release from prison. At Acts (7.25) the same word is used of the Exodus: "God was giving them deliverance."

Salvation is sometimes spoken of as a present possession. In the one passage in the Gospels where Jesus uses the word, he says to penitent Zacchaeus: "Today salvation has come to this house" (Luke 19.9). It was not something for which Zacchaeus had to wait. It was not something which would be bestowed at death nor yet something upon which he could enter only in the hereafter. He already had it. It is sometimes spoken of, however, as a goal toward which one must strive. Paul writes to the Philippians (2.12): "work out your own salvation with fear and trembling." In I Peter (2.2) it is spoken of as something toward which one develops: "Like newborn babes, long for the pure spiritual milk, that by it you may grow up to salvation." The New Testament teaching on this matter is summed up in I Peter (1.9): "As the outcome of your faith you obtain the salvation of your souls."

In Luke's account of Jesus' dealing with sin and disease, the same Greek words are, in the King James Bible, translated in two different ways. At Luke (7.50) his message to the sinful woman in Simon's house is: "Thy faith has saved thee: go in peace." At Luke (8.48) his words to the sick woman who confidently reached out and touched him in the crowd: "Thy faith hath made thee whole: go in peace." The Greek in these two passages is absolutely identical. The RE-VISED STANDARD VERSION also translates them differently: "Your faith has saved you," "Your faith has made you well." The translators felt that the rendering needed to suit the context. To be delivered from sin is to be saved. To be delivered from disease is to get well. In the shipwreck passage in Acts, the King James has Paul urging people to eat for reasons of health: "Wherefore I pray you take *some* meat; for this is for your health" (Acts 27.34).

All this helps to bring out the fact that the true significance of salvation is deliverance—deliverance from whatever threatens. If it is a shipwreck which impends, salvation will take one form. If it is a long prison term which stretches out before one, salvation will be of a different sort. If disease hangs on, salvation will mean still something else. It is important that misconceptions of salvation, and conceptions not based on the Bible, should be cleared up.

Note, for example, that in the New Testament it is bodies and not souls which are described as being in hell. Picturing the urgent necessity of letting nothing stand in the way of all-out devotion to God's cause Jesus says: "If your right eye causes you to sin, pluck it out and throw it away; it is better that you lose one of your members than that your whole"— what, soul? no—"body be thrown into hell. And if your right hand causes you to sin, cut it off and throw it away; it is better that you lose one of your members than that your whole body go into hell" (Mt. 5.29f).

In our Lord's parable of the Rich Man and Lazarus, the "rich man also died and was buried" (Luke 16.22). It is nowhere said that his soul went to hell. It is said that "in Hades, being in torment, he lifted up his eyes." Do souls have eyes? And why does he want Lazarus to come? "To dip the end of his finger in water and cool my tongue" (Luke 16.24). Do souls have tongues? And can they be soothed with moist fingers?

On one occasion, Jesus does say, according to Matthew (10.28): "And do not fear those who kill the body but cannot kill the soul; rather fear him who can destroy both soul and body in hell." This is admittedly a difficult saying. Who is it that has power to "destroy both soul and body in hell"? The reporters do not tell us, and perhaps some familiar idea at the time made it clear to the original hearers. In any case, some say it is God, others that it is the devil. This is almost the only passage in the New Testament (with the possible exception of Luke 14.33 and 16.1) which can be attributed either to God or to the devil.

The reference, however, seems to be to God, since nowhere else in the New Testament are we bidden to fear the devil. We are bidden to resist him and courageously to defy him (James 4.17; I Peter 5.9), but not to fear him. Although the evil one tries to drag us down to Gehenna, he has no authority to send us there.

Jesus is here urging his friends to faithful witness-bearing. They must have the courage of their convictions. The Pharisees may threaten their lives, but their souls are in God's hands. The warning, "fear him who, after he has killed, has power to cast into hell," is aimed primarily at those who are enemies of the truth, but Jesus' friends also must take it to heart. If fear seals their lips and they remain silent when they ought to be making public confession, this places their own spiritual life in danger. Jesus goes on to base this appeal for faithful testimony on the infinite love God has for each individual: "Are not five sparrows sold for two pennies? And not one of them is forgotten before God. Why, even the hairs of your head are all numbered" (Luke 12.6f).

Whatever the difficulties in the passage, however, it is not said that God condemns the soul to eternal torment in hell. It is said that he may *destroy* (ἀπολέσαι) both soul and body in hell." The Talmud relates that "the school of Shammai taught that at the judgment day there would be three classes of men. Of them, 1 would remain in Gehenna for 12 months, after which their bodies would be destroyed and their souls burned."

Matthew (25.31-46) gives a frightful picture of the doom that awaits the wicked: "Depart from me, you cursed, into eternal fire prepared for the devil and his angels." Several things need to be said about this: To begin with, the invidious distinction which we make between the sheep and the goats is not in the parable, nor in Oriental life. "The goat was not in evil repute in the East, as contrasted to the sheep; on the contrary, the he-goat was a symbol of dignity, so that the point of the analogy is merely the separation. The sheep and the goats are always seen together under the same shepherd and in company; yet they never trespass on the domain of each other."

The next thing that needs to be said is that the picture which Jesus uses of eternal fire is not original with him and is evidently not intended to convey any special teaching. It is simply an adaptation by him of a passage from the pseudepigraphical literature familiar to his hearers. Enoch (10.13) says: "they (evil angels) will be led off to the abyss of fire" and Secrets of Enoch (10.4-6) says: "this place is prepared for those who do not honor God;—and for them this place is prepared as an eternal inheritance."

Again, it must be noted that it is not souls but nations which are thus condemned. Jewish thought envisioned a time of judgment when everybody would be judged by the standard of right which they knew. At that time, Psalm 9:17 has it:

> "The wicked shall depart to Sheol,
>   all the nations that forget God."

Here, then, is Jesus' picture of God's judgment upon the nation. It is not a picture of individual souls burning for ever in torment.

Finally, it has to be noted why the nations are punished or

rewarded. Is it because they either neglected their souls or "saved" their souls? Rather it must be said that only those souls were saved who forget themselves in ministering to another's needs: "I was hungry and you gave me food, I was thirsty and you gave me drink, I was a stranger and you welcomed me. I was naked and you clothed me, I was sick and you visited me, I was in prison and you came to me" (Mt. 25.35f).

In Luke (19.10) Jesus gives us the purpose of his coming: "For the Son of Man came to seek and to save the lost." The concluding phrase, in the Greek, is a neuter singular. It says, "what is lost." Salvation is for all lost things. The 15th chapter of Luke, with its stories of the lost sheep, the lost coin, and the lost boy, helps us to understand the saying of William Temple that the principal characteristic of God is a concern for lost things. Wherever there is anything that is lost, Christ came to save it. This applies to lost ambition, lost energy, lost time, lost talents, lost economic systems, lost civilizations.

In the south, the problem of getting rid of cotton seed was a difficult one. Great piles of them were allowed to rot on the ground, and this necessitated legislation prohibiting the pollution of water supplies. These huge quantities of seed were an enormous waste until men found out how they could be put to work. They are now used in our kitchens as shortening, as salad oil, and for deep frying. They are used in the manufacture of soap, washing powder, cosmetics, artificial leather, and a hundred other things.

Cotton seed, once wasted, are the basis of many an industry. Best of all, there is no longer any problem of what to do with them. The demand for cotton seed actually became so great that the farmers could not keep up with it. When it was found that peanuts contained even richer quantities of the same oil, many farmers turned to raising peanuts. As with cotton seed, so with the great heaps of waste there are in human life. They cease to burden when they are put to work in a great cause. Salvation is the comprehensive miracle by which wasted lives and fragments of lives are made over. Jesus came to seek and to save everything that was lost. This puts a premium upon redeeming all we can of our own lives.

24. Gaining Our Lives

A mother who was brought up to know and love the King James Bible was fond of saying to her children, "Possess your souls in patience!" This advice she would offer whenever they seemed too much in a hurry: when they could not wait for Christmas to come or vacation to begin or supper to be served. It is an allusion to Luke (21.19): "In your patience possess ye your souls" (KJV). The assumption seems to be that one should so permeate his soul with quiet resignation so that he would be able uncomplainingly to endure delay and disappointment. There is something to be said for this. God seems never to be in a hurry, and we can cause ourselves a good deal of chafing and misery by trying to outrun Him.

RSV, however, gives a rather different twist to these words: "By your endurance you will gain your lives." The three principal words all are different: "endurance" instead of "patience," "gain" instead of "possess," "lives" instead of "souls." Patience is a word that got into our English versions by way of the Latin. In Galatians (5.22) Paul says that, among the fruits of the Spirit, is what KJV calls "long-suffering"; RSV renders it by "patience." The word here used means submission to injuries without paying back.

The word used in our passage, however, is a different word. It means endurance of suffering without giving way. It is the word used to describe the virtue shown by martyrs. The verb from which this noun is derived occurs in the Gospels: "He who endures to the end will be saved" (Mark 13.13 cf. Mt. 10.22; 24.13). It happens, however, that the Latin has but a single word, *patientia,* to translate these two different ideas. Under the influence of the Vulgate, therefore, the KJ translators here used "patience" where "endurance" is now required. The point is that the Christian's weapon is endurance, not violence.

By steadfastness under affliction the Christians will "gain" their lives. Webster gives as one meaning of "possess": "To gain, seize, obtain, win." This meaning, however, he describes as "archaic." It is the meaning which the King James intended to convey. At Luke (18.12) KJV has the Pharisee boasting: "I give tithes of all that I possess." Now a man does not pay tithes of what he possesses, or holds as property. If he did that, his resources would be constantly dwindling. It is not a man's capital but his income which he tithes. RSV translates this passage: "I give tithes of all that I get."

Actually the word in Greek is a commercial term which suggests doing business in the market place, acquiring, getting, purchasing, buying. In Acts 1.18 (*cf.* 8.20) it is used of Judas who "bought a field with the reward of his wickedness." It is as if our lives did not belong to us, and the only way we can win them is to pay the purchase price—in this case, unending endurance of wrong. Mary Ellen Chase says of Abby Aldrich Rockefeller (Foreword to the Biography) that she regarded life "as a loan and not as a mere possession." Of some one inordinately beholden to another we say: "He cannot call his soul his own." A Christian cannot call his soul his own either. It is lent him by Another. By patient endurance he may gain the mastery over it, but self-mastery of this type is Christ-mastery.

Christians thus hope to gain their "lives." The Greek word here is the one from which we get the first two syllables of "psychology." "Psyche" in the New Testament is used of "whatever is felt to belong most essentially to man's life, when his bodily life has come to be regarded as a secondary thing." One modern lexicographer thinks "it comes near the modern conception, *self*." In a number of places in the New Testament (Acts 2.41; 7.14; 27.37; I Peter 3.20) it is used with a cardinal numeral, suggesting that it may have been the word for "persons" in formal documents, such as census rolls. In any case, here is the assurance that by patient endurance to the end, the Christian will be able to save his true self, whatever else he may lose.

The *psyche* is the seat of the feelings, desires, affections. In one of the songs of Christmas Mary said:

"My soul magnifies the Lord" (Luke 1.46).

The Fourth Gospel represents Jesus as saying, during the last week of his earthly life, "Now is my soul troubled. And what shall I say . . .?" (John 12.27). To the waiting friends in Gethsemane he said: "My soul is very sorrowful, even to death; remain here, and watch" (Mark 14.34). In this connection there are three occurrences of the word *psyche* where it is translated "heart": "Doing the will of God from the heart" (Eph. 6.6); "so that you may not grow weary or fainthearted" (Heb. 12.3); "Whatever your task, work heartily, as serving the Lord and not men" (Col. 3.23).

The word *psyche* is sometimes used in compounds to suggest that it is the seat of personality difficulties. At I Thess. 5.14 there is a reference to what the Greek literally describes as "little-souled people." The King James Version translates the compound as "the feeble-minded." "Feeble-minded," however, is a term that has taken on a specialized significance in the twentieth-century age of measurement. Those with a low I.Q. are the feeble-minded. This reference has nothing to do with mental capacity, but describes rather those who easily grew despondent and wondered whether it was longer worth while to try to live by their high convictions. The REVISED STANDARD VERSION translates the word by "faint-hearted."

Twice in the Epistle of James (1.8 and 4.8) there is reference to what the Greek describes as "two-souled people." "Double-minded" is the conventional English rendering: "For that person must not suppose that a double-minded man unstable in all his ways, will receive anything from the Lord" (1.8). "Cleanse your hands, you sinners, and purify your hearts, you men of double mind" (4.8). Side by side with this we need to place James 1:6: "he who doubts is like a wave of the sea that is driven and tossed by the wind." When a little girl was wavering in the matter of an important decision, her mother said: "Now, Mary, you must make up your mind." "But, mother," protested the child, "it is easy enough for you to make up your mind. You have only one mind to make up. I have a lot of minds."

The natural man does have a lot of minds—the desire to outdo his fellows, the desire for fame, the desire for riches, the desire for business success and social approval, as well as the desire to do what his conscience tells him is right and win the favor of those whom he really admires. He is pulled hither and thither by these conflicting desires—and it is no wonder his body gets battered and bruised in the process. The cure for double-mindedness is the kind of sincerity of purpose and single-hearted devotion which can be summed up in the word integrity. The word integrity is built up from the Latin word for entire. It means "state or quality of being complete, undivided, or unbroken." Psychology seeks for integration of the personality—that is to say, a restoration of the wholeness.

The Scriptural word for us at this point is 2 Corinthians (11.3) where Paul warns lest "your thoughts will be led astray from a sincere and pure devotion to Christ." The King James Version at this point reads: "so your minds should be corrupted from the simplicity that is in Christ." The latter phrase "the simplicity that is in Christ" has been used to oppose theological learning. Simplicity, however, is here used as the opposite of "duplicity." The REVISED STANDARD VERSION makes it clear that this is not a reference to such things as might appeal to a simpleton, but rather to such things as are unmixed, sincere. The cure for instability is "sincere and pure devotion to Christ."

In Bunyan's allegory, Pilgrim and Hopeful are the prisoners of Giant Despair in Doubting Castle. They suppose that they can never better their condition. The doors seem securely locked and Giant amuses himself by torturing them. They consider whether they would not rather die. "My soul chooseth strangling rather than life," says Christian, "and the grave is more easy for me than this dungeon." But wiser counsel prevails. Presently they find themselves released, and stronger for the rest of their journey. So it is ever that by manly endurance men gain their own lives.

And whenever this happens, of course, it is for always. There is no loss but only gain in the discovery that the emphasis in the Bible is upon gaining our lives rather than upon saving our souls. Ultimately, however, it may all come to the same thing. Science has taught us to think in terms of the conservation of energy. In a universe where physical energy, in spite of the changes it may undergo, can never be lost, is it conceivable that God would allow the personalities dear to Him to end in nothingness? The preservation of values here is indicated by better translation of a familiar passage.

In the REVISED STANDARD VERSION, Abigail says to David: "If men rise up to pursue you and to seek your life, the life of my lord shall be bound in the bundle of the living in the care of the LORD your God" (I Sam. 25.29). The picture is that of treasured possessions carefully wrapped together in order that they may be safely carried on the person. This is a practice still common in the east, and in it many parallels to the life of man are discerned. In India a just judge is said to be bound in the bundle of righteousness, and a lover in the bundle of love. By her use of the simile, Abigail intends to express the hope that, under God's protection, David's life may be spared.

The King James Version at this point reads: "Yet a man is risen to pursue thee, and to seek thy soul: but the soul of my lord shall be bound in the bundle of life with the Lord thy God." Commentators formerly deduced from this that the passage is "one of the earliest and most definite expressions of a sure belief in an eternal future in the presence of God." The Hebrew word here is the one which occurs in Genesis (2.7), and in both cases the proper rendering is "life" rather than "soul." The reference here is to "the safe preservation of the righteous on this earth in the grace and fellowship of the Lord." By extension, however, on the principle of Philippians (1.6), this may be thought of as applying to the life of the ages. Paul there writes of his conviction that "he who began a good work in you will bring it to completion." So here, to quote a German commentator, "whoever is so hidden in the gracious fellowship of the Lord in this life, that no enemy can harm him or injure his life, the Lord will not allow to perish, even though temporal death should come." It is good to know that in this relationship, too, man is not alone.

It is in fellowship that another of religion's greatest blessings opens to us.

25. Confess to One Another

A missionary to India tells of a Hindu doctor, interested in problems of mental health, who was won to Christianity because, as he puts it, "Jesus connected the forgiveness of sins and the healing of disease." This, he held, was sound. The Epistle of James—containing so many echoes of the Sermon on the Mount that many believe it to have been written by the brother of Jesus, though the author himself claims no more than that he is "a servant of God and of the Lord Jesus Christ" (James 1.1)—clarifies the relationship: "Therefore confess your sins to one another, and pray for one another, that you may be healed" (James 5.16).

This is a reminder that healing of the body may involve the whole person, and is therefore something that cannot take place in isolation. This is to be taken into account in evaluating the claims of those who make a daily offer of healing miracles. It is the practice of some of these to have people line up and pass in front of the "healer"—and the television cameras!—for one brief moment. The "healer" seizes each patient and cries: "Be healed." The healing lines projected on the home television screen show an unbroken succession of miracles. It is not explained that the films are carefully edited to delete all the obvious failures, and are presented in such a way as to suggest that more is happening to the patient than a scientific observer at hand would be able to detect. Nor are we allowed to follow the patients as they return to their homes and find themselves the next day without the support of the healer's glib assurances.

Healers require those who wish to benefit from their min-

istry to form a line. So far as Scripture indicates, the simple
wish to get better is not the sole precondition of healing, nor
does the Scripture indicate that the healer is to lay hands indiscriminately upon all who come. One of Jesus' parables
relates that a king "gave a marriage feast for his son ... But
when the king came in to look at the guests, he saw there a
man who had no wedding garment; and he said to him,
'Friend, how did you get in here without a wedding garment?' And he was speechless. Then the king said to the attendants, 'Bind him hand and foot, and cast him into the
outer darkness'" (Mt. 22.2, 11-13).

In the realm of healing, as in all else that concerns the real
life of man, there is such a thing as dressing for the occasion.
The beginning of Job's acceptance by the Lord comes when
he says:

> "I despise myself,
> and repent in dust and ashes" (Job 42.6).

This is rather different from the carnival atmosphere of the
healer's tent where the line moves slowly forward in saw-
dust and kleig lights. The healing forces which God releases
through his servants does not work magically. Rather are
they bound up with what Paul calls "godly grief" which
"produces a repentance that leads to salvation and brings no
regret" (2 Cor. 7.10).

One in this mood must have some one to share it, and
Scripture recommends the confessional. We are to confess
our sins. The King James Bible at this point reads: "Confess
your faults one to another." The Greek word however is a
characteristic New Testament word for sin. It means missing
the mark. It is a term that might be used in archery. You set
up a target and aim at it, but something goes wrong and you
do not hit it. Perhaps your missile falls short; perhaps it strays
to one side or the other. In any case, you miss the mark.

And that is one Scriptural picture of sin. God, so to speak, has given us something to shoot at, but we fail to hit it; "all have sinned," says Paul (Romans 3.23), "and fall short of the glory of God." "All we like sheep have gone astray," says the prophet (Is. 53.6); "we have turned every one to his own way." We have erred, failed, done wrong. All this is sin. As one of the Reformation catechisms has it, sin is "any want of conformity unto, or transgression of, the law of God."

Every man knows in his heart that he has missed the mark, and we are to confess our sins. To confess our sins is to acknowledge them, to own them and admit that they are ours. The beginning of forgiveness is the admission that we have done wrong: "if we say we have no sin we deceive ourselves, and the truth is not in us" (I John 1.8). The chances are that on matters of this kind we shall deceive nobody but ourselves —we shall surely not fool our neighbors! Nor can we deceive God: "If we say we have not sinned, we make him a liar, and his word is not in us" (I John 1.10). There is no one from whom we can hide it except ourselves, and if we do that it will be like a poison which can find no outlet but will go on corrupting the whole body. No one can hope for health who denies to himself that he is in need of healing.

We must therefore confess our sins. And we are to confess *our* sins. It is much easier to confess other people's sins than our own. Much of daily conversation consists of confessing the sins of other people. But this can do them no good, and will do harm to ourselves. The confession of their sins must be left to them. What we have to do is to confess our own. Jesus told of two men who "went up into the temple to pray, one a Pharisee and the other a tax collector. The Pharisee stood and prayed thus with himself, 'God, I thank thee that I am not like other men, extortioners, unjust, adulterers, or even like this tax collector. I fast twice a week, I give tithes of all that I get.' But the tax collector, standing far off, would not even lift up his eyes to heaven, but beat his breast, saying, 'God, be merciful to me a sinner!' I tell you, this man went down to his house justified rather than the other" (Luke 18.10-14).

"Confess your sins," says James, "one to another." This suggests the intimate nature of the Christian fellowship. James is not here advising us to go out on the street and confess our sins to the first person we meet, nor to some chance companion of our journey. He is addressing the Christian community. He specifically mentions the elders of the church. The thought is, of course, that the warmth and sympathy of the community of believers forms the climate in which confession can do its healing work. Doctors tell us that in the treatment of disease atmospheric conditions may have a determining effect. If you have sinus trouble they send you away from a damp and foggy region: What you need is sunshine and clear air. If we have sinned, we need to breathe the bracing air of the Christian community. We ought to be so close to our brethren that it will be entirely natural to confess our sins to them.

"Confess your faults one to another." The Protestant conception of the confessional is that the church is an association of like-minded people, so cordial in their fellowship, that, when one member does wrong, he will find himself spontaneously confessing to his brethren. But it is upon the basis of this text that the Roman church has built up its idea of the confessional. Their interpretation seems to us a great perversion of the simple words of Scripture. It does not say that we ought to confess our sins to a priest; it says we ought to confess them to one another. A brief bit of history will enable us to understand how this came about. It was not until the Fourth Lateran Council, in the year 1215, that annual confession to a priest became obligatory. In the early church the confession seems to have been to the entire congregation. Tertullian tells us that forgiveness for sin was possible "only after a humiliating public confession; the penitent was bidden to feed prayers on fastings, to groan, to weep and make outcries unto the Lord your God; to bow before the feet of the presbyters, and kneel to God's dear ones."

There plainly was a danger here. We can imagine the sensation that was created in the congregation when some respected member of it stood up and confessed to murder or theft or harlotry. The shock of it would plainly not have left the rest in a worshipful mood, to say the least. Also, such a procedure might actually become itself a school of crime; We know that one of the worst things about sending boys to penal institutions, whether reformatories or jails, is that in them they learn how to do a lot of crimes they had not thought of before. It is entirely possible that lurid confession to a congregation might open up new avenues of sin to innocent members of the group; and the plea for forgiveness would thus become a temptation to others. It was to avoid this that the church wisely began to have confessions made, not in public, but in private, and gradually the type of confession you now get in the Roman church became a rule.

The dangers in public confession are evident to any one who has followed the technique used by Frank Buchman and his so-called Oxford Group movement. Among them, public confession is the rule. At some houseparty or in the ballroom of some hotel a man discloses his past to the assembled company. Buchman makes a great point of getting what he calls interesting sinners. The more unconventional things a man has done, within the limits of social respectability, the more sought after he is. The younger and more innocent members of the group listen with bated breath and popping eyes to the revelations of his past. The tendency is for the next person to try to confess something even worse, and the thing becomes, not a confessional, but a tall story club. Also, the "interesting sinner" is encouraged to tell his story time and time again. It never loses anything in the telling, and becomes an end in itself. The narrator is very proud to have so black a past.

All this, of course, is a great perversion of the simple act of spiritual cleansing described in the Scripture. We are bidden to confess our sins, assured that when we do God will forgive them. He not only forgives but forgets. We are told that He puts them as far from Him as the East is from the West. And if He does that, we have no right to keep dragging them up again, much less to repeat them so often they become something about which to boast. One has heard of a young lady who went to the Catholic confessional. She said: "Father, I have something to confess: a young man kissed me last night." "And how many times did the young man kiss you?" asked the priest. "Now Father," she said, "I came to confess, not to boast." The Roman church makes the confessional private and formal. Frank Buchman makes it public and enticing. The two are equally far from the simple New Testament act of finding somebody in the Christian community who will be kind and sympathetic, and then confessing our sins one to another. Nobody then can afford to go it alone in life.

26. Not Good If Detached

Many years ago, Carlyle wrote in *Sartor Resartus*: "There is not a red Indian, hunting by Lake Winnipeg, can quarrel with his squaw, but the whole world must suffer for it: will not the price of beaver rise? It is a mathematical fact," he continued, "that the casting of this pebble from my hand alters the center of gravity of the Universe." The mutual interdependence of people in the twentieth century world is even more apparent, but the underlying truth has never been better expressed than in 1 Corinthians (12.14, 26). "For the body does not consist of one member but of many . . . If one member suffers, all suffer together; if one member is honored, all rejoice together."

Originally spoken of the distinctively Christian fellowship which is called the church, the words imply that any one who cuts himself off from others ceases to be a part of life's organism. A British social scientist believes that many persons move to the suburbs or barricade themselves in housing developments "endeavoring to combat the pain and embarrassment of unwanted social contacts by blocking them out." "Why is it," he asked, "that mankind seems to be trying to shelter behind net curtains, a large aspidistra and the china dog?" Such retreat and withdrawal betoken a form of loneliness which may manifest itself in mental illness. It has been found, on the other hand, that strong identification with religious and ethnic groups makes for individual acceptance and sound mental health. A study was made of eight nationality groups, including 170,000 people, in the east midtown section of New York. Those who since early childhood had identified themselves with ethnic and religious groups were found to have achieved "integrated adjustment and sound mental health."

The sustaining power of the group is brilliantly exemplified by a fellowship designed for those who have a peculiar type of need. The very genius of Alcoholics Anonymous is that in togetherness there is strength. Members of the A. A. have all been redeemed from bondage to strong drink, and are kept from backsliding by the knowledge that others are with them and for them. Each member carries in his pocket a card. He agrees that, before taking a drink, he will take out that card and write down on it his reasons for doing so, reasons to be presented to the entire group at the next meeting. This, of course, is a strong deterrent. The knowledge that others expect him not to fail is an aid in keeping the pledge. This is certainly an illustration of the power of fellowship to preserve and restore.

Other aspects of A. A. illustrate Scriptural truths. Any one who becomes a member becomes also an evangelist. The very condition of his belonging is that he will go out and win other converts by imparting to them the good news. A. A. again, is proud of the fact that all sorts of people are in its make-up. A pastor, invited to one of the meetings, was astonished to find among those present a man who lived across the street from him, the father of playmates of his children, and a barber who had a shop near his church. A. A. is proud that it has chauffeurs and laborers as well as professors and millionaires. Whether it admits it or not, whether it recognizes it or not, the organization thus exhibits many characteristics of Biblical religion and furnishes contemporary evidence that people together can do better things than people individually.

The Menninger Foundation, in Topeka, Kans., represents this feeling of togetherness as applied to the realm of medicine. Its founder was a country doctor, C. F. Menninger, who took his sons into partnership as soon as they had received the kind of training that had not been available in his own youth. When the new hospital was opened in 1955, there were 175 psychiatric specialists and 225 other workers at the Foundation.

When Dr. C. F. Menninger was asked why he preferred a clinic to single practice, he replied: "Why do football players put their heads together in a huddle? To outline procedure and to win."

In our national capital there are two obstetricians who have pooled their practice. Prospective mothers who come to either of them must agree that, if necessary, the other may deliver the baby. That is to say, the doctors have agreed that each may have a day off now and again, with complete freedom from telephone calls. The other doctor will respond to every summons. Both are able to do their work better. Both also are able, in their free time, to identify themselves with the interests of their own family, church, and community.

It is the sense of belonging to a group which sustains men amid the dangers and difficulties of war. A chaplain in the Second World War reports that he asked men what it was that kept them going in times of crisis. In no case did the answer have to do with ideology. No one was sustained by the desire to preserve democracy, or maintain the American way of life, nor even by abstract love of country. What made them fight on, they said, was unwillingness to let other people down. Their buddies were counting on them, and to this trust they must at all hazards be faithful. United States military authorities are now seeking to build upon this sense of loyalty to the group. In military assignments, men have been shunted around with no consideration as to where they have been or with whom they have been. Soldiers are now to be assigned, so far as possible, to four-man teams. These four men are expected to find each other toward the end of the basic training period. They will be sent overseas together. "Not only will the men team up in the field, in mess halls and at training sites, but they will be permitted to arrange their quarters so that their bunk spaces are together." Even en route to duty outside the country, this fellowship is to be carefully preserved. While the men are quartered on troop ships, officers are to see to it that "all four-man teams are physically located aboard ship in a manner sufficient to maintain easy communication within the company and the integrity of each four-man team."

A crying need of our time is that this insight should now be applied to the modern industrial situation. A man who appeared on a television program was asked his occupation. He said "Hobo." He went on to distinguish between a hobo and a bum. A bum, he said, will never work. A hobo will work occasionally, in order that he may provide himself the means for travel and sustenance. When asked about his past life, the hobo said that he had a college education but that he preferred the life of a wanderer to that of a factory worker. Long before assembly line techniques had reduced man's significance to that of a cog in a machine, Nietzsche said that Napoleon was not a butcher but a benefactor. He gave men the glory of dying on the battlefield rather than the attrition of making another million collar buttons.

Another participant in a television program was asked whether she was a housewife. She said no, that she worked for a well known tire and rubber company. To the question, "what do you do?" she answered, "make airplane parts." When pressed for an explanation, she said that vast rolls of material are stretched out on a long table. When inquiry was made as where the rolls of material come from, she had no other answer than: "From the warehouse." She then described her part in an impersonal process. She had a pattern which she placed on the material and cut around it. To the question, "What is the design used for?" she said, "I haven't the faintest idea." When asked what she did with the design when she had cut it out, she replied: "I hand it on to the next girl."

The question then was: "What does the next girl do with it?" "She punches holes in it." "What are the holes for?" "I haven't the slightest idea." No one could ever develop a sense of significant achievement in a position like that. Dr. Will Menninger declares that "The most important job satisfaction depends on each one having the chance to develop the kind of relationship with his associates that will result in mutual respect and confidence. Achieving this calls for more people who are spiritually mature enough to replace the question, 'What's in it for me?' with 'What's in it for us?' and 'What should *I* do about it?'"

Near the end of his life, Dr. Felix Adler, founder of the Ethical Culture Movement, said: "I am grateful for the Idea that has used me." Dr. Harry Emerson Fosdick also, in his autobiography, *The Living of These Days*, has a chapter entitled "Ideas That Have Used Me." Such an approach to one's own life saves him from egotism, since it subordinates individual achievement to the causes he has served. While Adler gave thanks for one "Idea" that used him, Dr. Fosdick lists several by which he has been caught up. Although Dr. Fosdick was widely known as an opponent of fundamentalism, modernism as such he does not regard as among the ideas that have used him. Among the ones he does list are these: "Mankind desperately needs what Christianity at its best has to offer"; "The ultimate criterion of any civilization's success or failure is to be found in what happens to the underdog"; "Winning the war (in the words of the United States Defense Department) may well not be preserving national security"; that "mankind is inevitably becoming 'one world'" and that "Today being an internationalist is an essential part of being a patriot"; "We cannot meet communism's challenge by reactionary policies."

The twentieth century has moralistic arguments about why it is wrong to steal. It is not right to get something for nothing. It is not right to take what belongs to other people. The Ten Commandments are content with the forthright injunction, "You shall not steal" (Ex. 20.15). The New Testament, however, puts the whole thing in a rather different light. Ephesians (4.28) says: "Let the thief no longer steal, but rather let him labor, doing honest work with his hands, so that he may be able to give to those in need." Here is an interesting picture of life in the early Christian church, which was evidently already receiving into its fellowship persons for whom thievery had been a way of life.

The point here, however, is the motive enjoined for cessation from theft. Thieving is to be renounced so that the one-time thief, so far from living off of what belongs to others, will have something to contribute to others! We might have thought it a good thing for the thief to get a job in order that he could restore what he had wrongly taken from others. But the Scriptural doctrine goes far beyond the idea of mere restitution. If a man has a real concern about what he may be able to do for others, then thievery, as a way of life, will be for ever abandoned. Railway tickets often carry the words, "Not good if detached." The thief is cut off from his fellows. When he becomes interested in doing something for them, he ceases to be detached.

III. SPIRIT

27. Living Temples

The Scriptural attitude toward the body is rather different from that found in many of the ethnic faiths. Literature's best and most concise description of the pagan world is found in the first chapter of Romans, where Paul says of those who ignored the revelation of Himself which God had granted to them, "God gave them up in the lusts of their hearts to impurity, to the dishonoring of their bodies among themselves, because they exchanged the truth about God for a lie and worshiped and served the creature rather than the Creator, who is blessed for ever!" (Rom. 1.24f). In contrast with the abuses to which pagans subject their bodies, Paul in the same letter, says to the Christians: "I appeal to you ... by the mercies of God, to present your bodies as a living sacrifice, holy and acceptable to God, which is your spiritual worship" (Rom. 12.1).

To the Corinthians he says "glorify God in your body" (1 Cor. 6.20). The reason he gives is this: "You are not your own; you were bought with a price." If we have the use of a lawn mower, an automobile, or a pair of scissors that belongs to somebody else, we take better care of it than if it belonged to ourselves. So, says Paul, our bodies are not our own and we must treat them with the respect and care due to another's property. "It's my life," we are apt to say, "and I can do what I want with it," or, "It's my life and I intend to live it." These are very human expressions which sometimes represent a quite justifiable revolt against some of the holds that would hold us, but it is not Scriptural language. "You are not your own; you were bought with a price."

When we stop to think of it, we realize that everything we have was bought with a price. We were not called into being suddenly. Our physical bodies were bought with a price which only mothers can reckon up. Our education may have been handed to us on a silver platter—but somebody had to pay for it. It was bought with a price of toil and sacrifice and anxiety which fathers gladly paid.

Many look back upon the time when physicians and nurses saved bodies from going to pieces. Medical skill, so freely bestowed, was not easily won. Long years of devoted study enabled them to save life. Most of what we are and have was bought with a price—and the price was paid by others. If we had paid for all these items ourselves, then we might boast that our lives were our own. But life takes on a different aspect when it dawns upon us that the things we enjoy were bought and paid for by other people.

Still another reason why the body must be highly regarded is found in Paul's Corinthian correspondence: "Do you not know," he asks (1 Cor. 6.19), "that your body is a temple of the Holy Spirit within you, which you have from God?" Corinth was noted for its pagan temples. The worship of two heathen deities was localized there, and each had a magnificent temple: Poseidon, god of the sea, called Neptune by the Romans; and Aphrodite, goddess of beauty, called Venus by the Romans. Christian architecture had no temples to rival these. In fact, Christians of that era had no special buildings of any kind in which to worship. They simply met in the houses of the members. Colossians (4.15), Philemon 2 and Romans 16.5 mention the church in the house. Acts (2.46) says of the early Christians: "breaking bread in their homes, they partook of food with glad and generous hearts." It was not until several generations later that separate buildings were erected for Christian worship.

The Christians did not need to feel inferior. They had no resources to build temples of stone adorned with gold. They had even more magnificent temples, and Paul reminds each one: "your body is a temple of the Holy Spirit." Even irreligious people respect a house of worship. People who smoke while shaving and smoke while dining and smoke while making love would not think of smoking in the sanctuary of God. Delinquent boys who throw stones through windows are not apt to smash stained glass. Thieves who break into vacant houses to steal the plumbing hesitate to do that to a place held sacred. Reverence for God's house is felt even by those who deny that they are religious.

The human body is as sacred as a church—and for the same reason: both are temples of the Most High. "There is but one temple in the Universe," says the devout European poet and romanticist, Novalis, "and that is the Body of Man. Nothing is holier than that high form. Bending before men is a reverence done to this Revelation in the Flesh. We touch Heaven when we lay our hands on a human body." A book entitled *The Care of God's House* (by Irene Caudwell; Morehouse-Gorham, 1948) tells when and how to sweep the church, clean the windows, care for the altar cloth. This is helpful to altar guilds as well as to sextons. Paul indicates the care we are to take of God's other temple.

Primitive man has not unnaturally felt that the power of procreation was in some way linked with the power of creation. Many ethnic faiths, therefore, have had fertility rites. Barren women would go to the temple and lie with the priest, in order that the god might induce pregnancy. Cult prostitution was a regular feature of pagan worship and the temple of Aphrodite in Corinth actually had a thousand such women in its sacred precincts. But that does not accord with the

Scriptural view of marriage and it is to the people in Corinth that Paul writes: "Do you not know that your bodies are members of Christ? Should I therefore take the members of Christ and make them members of a prostitute? Never! Do you not know that he who joins himself to a prostitute becomes one body with her?" (1 Cor. 6.15f).

How strangely contradictory is our attitude toward the worth of a human body! If one human body gets trapped in a coal mine, buried in a snowdrift, or lost on a mountainside, men will spare no expense—they will move heaven and earth —to rescue it. On the other hand men will profess a certain delight if a hundred thousand bodies are destroyed in a single night—provided those hundred thousand are in an "enemy" land. We use the airplane to rush serum across a continent to save the life of a small boy, and employ the same machine to rain death indiscriminately upon men, women, and children—noncombatants all. A great surgeon will sacrifice everything to make himself a more effective healer of the human body, and the man of sordid tastes will look upon the human body as something to exploit in a side show.

Some men pay more attention to the fine points of horse-flesh than to keeping their own bodies in good condition. Some, on the other hand, make of their bodies a cult. In the average drugstore there are said to be 58 brands of tooth-paste and powder, 111 kinds of cold cream, 44 brands of hair tonic—most of them worthless, many of them actually harmful. In Philippians (3.19) Paul speaks sorrowfully of some whose "end is destruction, their god is the belly, and they glory in their shame, with minds set on earthly things." Gustatory delight seemed to dominate the thoughts of many Americans invalided home during the Second World War. Two of the things most wanted were "sufficient candy to make ourselves sick" and the chance to eat homemade cake "until we feel as if we are going to burst." One young man in those days, upon being asked what he was fighting for, replied that he was fighting for the good old American right to eat apple pie. Gluttons were placed by Dante in the third circle of hell.

On this point Paul is sure that whether we eat or drink, we should do it to the glory of God. We must be careful about what we bring into these living temples!

Charles H. Spurgeon, the great Baptist Evangelistic preacher, once declared that when he smoked, he smoked to the glory of God. When he was challenged on that point, he said: "When I have found intense pain relieved, a weary brain soothed, and calm, refreshing sleep obtained by a cigar, I have felt grateful to God and have blessed His Name: this is what I meant, and by no means did I use sacred words triflingly." He went on to add, however: "If through smoking I had wasted an hour of my time—if I had rendered my mind less vigorous—I trust I should see my fault and turn from it."

There is on sale at a tobacconist's in Scotland, "Dr. White's Glasgow Presbyterian Mixture." One of the curious things about our time is that our advertisers try to make us believe that their particular brand of tobacco has been relieved of its "tobacco-ness." In enjoining tobacco companies from making false claims, the Federal Trade Commission handed down an order stating that smoke from all leading brands is irritating to the mucous membranes of the respiratory tract, and that all leading brands contain plenty of nicotine and throat irritants. There is no appreciable difference in the effect upon the throat, nor in the amount of coughing produced. It was also found that, of 440 persons held to smoke one brand exclusively, more than a hundred did not do so, and many never touched it.

We ought not to be victimized by specious claims charmingly presented over radio or television, nor to be in bondage to any habit that dominates our lives. Peter says (2 Peter 2.19): "whatever overcomes a man, to that he is enslaved." So many have been enslaved by tobacco, that Herbert Brean has written a book called *How to Stop Smoking*. Smoking can be a sociable kind of thing. On the other hand, one has known some so enslaved to it that they continued to make their chests more hollow while having no money for books or for wholesome, constructive recreation.

In June, 1956, the American Cancer Society, the National Cancer Institute, the American Heart Association and the National Heart Institute organized the Study Group on Smoking and Health. The Study Group, composed of seven medical specialists, surveyed sixteen independent studies carried on in five countries and concluded that "there is a statistical association between smoking and the occurrence of lung cancer." Analysis indicates that, of men who smoke more than two packs a day, one in ten will die of lung cancer; among nonsmokers the incidence is estimated at one in 275. The evidence for correlation here is so strong, the group said, as to suggest "the initiation of public health measures ... Although the statistical evidence has often been quoted as indicating an association between heavy smoking and lung cancer, there is no evidence of a threshold level below which the risk disappears ... the lung cancer risk is statistically significant for half-pack-a-day-smokers."

Affirming that "the smoking of tobacco, particularly in the form of cigarettes, is an important health hazard," the Group indicated the finding of "statistical association" also between tobacco and "a number of other disease entities, including carcinoma of the larynx, oral cavity, esophagus, bladder, and stomach; peptic ulcer, bronchitis and tuberculosis; and thromboangitis obliterans." The uses to which we put the human body must always be settled with reference to the fact that it is "a temple of the Holy Spirit." He who knows this is better prepared to appreciate the way in which God deals with His people.

28. The Gift of Pain

One way of describing a healthy, happy baby is to say that he "never cries." Of course he cries sometimes: when a safety pin sticks him, when he is hungry, when he falls out of his crib. A certain amount of crying is good for him. When he first comes into the world, he must cry in order to fill his lungs with air, and the crying he subsequently does plays its part in the development of lung power. The Wisdom of Solomon (7.3f) represents Israel's greatest king as saying:

"when I was born, I began to breathe the common air,

. . . .

and my first sound was a cry like that of all."

In the 1940's a child was born who did not cry, because she was incapable of feeling pain. This is an exceedingly rare condition. It is congenital and apparently due to a defect in the central nervous system. No cure is known. The Ohio infant did not cry when she fell down. She did not cry when she bumped her head. She did not cry when she burned her hand on a hot stove. Doctors warned her parents that this "indifference to injury" was fraught with grave dangers for the child. She might break a bone and continue to use it until it was too late to set it properly. Should appendicitis develop, it might, without nature's usual warning of pain, become fatal before any one ever found out about it.

Spanking the child to warn her not to play with matches would do no good, since she could not feel the blows.

It takes an extreme case like this to make us realize that life without pain is not so desirable as it would seem. Pain has been defined as "the prayer of a nerve for blood that is pure." Within limits, this is biologically accurate. Pain is a friendly warning, like swinging red lights and a clanging gong at the railroad crossing. From a pinprick to an ache, pain stimulates reactions that enable us to draw away from danger.

It is impressive therefore to discover that Paul regards bodily suffering as something bestowed upon him as a result of God's gracious favor. That is the language he uses in 2 Corinthians (12.7): "a thorn was given me in the flesh." The word translated "was given" is the verb regularly used in the New Testament to describe the bestowal of God's favor. In Ephesians (3.8) Paul writes: "To me ... this grace was given, to preach to the Gentiles the unsearchable riches of Christ." The verb in the two sentences is precisely the same. In one and the same way Paul speaks of God's gracious favor in bestowing upon him a notable lifework as a preacher of the everlasting Gospel and in bestowing upon him a "thorn" in the flesh.

If it seems difficult to reconcile pain with the goodness of God, it must be recalled that men of the Bible endured physical agony—and wished to avoid it quite as much as we. In 2 Cor. (12.7) Paul tells us that "a thorn was given me in the flesh, a messenger of Satan, to harass me." He does not tell us the nature of his affliction—which is a remarkable commentary upon the character of Paul. We human beings are fond of talking about our operations—and a lesser man would surely have given us all the gory details. He does not even enumerate his symptoms. The one thing of which his brief description assures us is that it was painful. The Greek word translated "thorn" really means a pointed stick, the kind of sharpened pole with which stockades or picket fences are built, a device upon which human heads might be impaled. What Paul says is that he feels as if stakes were being driven into his body.

Some have given a mystical interpretation to this, supposing that Paul used a metaphor of physical suffering to describe mental anguish or spiritual torment. A wide variety of conjecture along this line has been evident. Some have thought it was remorse that he had spent so much of his life away from Christ and had once been a leader among those who "persecuted the church of God violently and tried to destroy it" (Gal. 1.13); some that the loneliness and hardship of travel, together with the opposition he so frequently encountered, were a constant temptation to give up his evangelistic and missionary work; some that fatigue and extreme depression of spirit brought on attacks of melancholia. In Philippians (3.5) he describes his own religious heritage: "a Hebrew born of Hebrews; as to the law a Pharisee." In Galatians (1.14) he writes: "I advanced in Judaism beyond many of my own age among my people so extremely jealous was I for the traditions of my fathers." That kind of birthright would surely tempt a man to pride. In a speech in his own defense before the magistrate, he tells how he was "brought up . . . at the feet of Gamaliel, educated according to the strict manner of the law of our fathers" (Acts 22.3). Gamaliel was a university professor noted for the breadth of his learning and the extent of his sympathies. From him Paul learned how to drink out of Greek vases as well as out of Jewish water jars. A man with that kind of educational background might be tempted to a feeling of superiority over his fellow-Christians, among whom "not many . . . were wise according to worldly standards, not many were powerful, not many were of noble birth" (1 Cor. 1.26).

Considering how unstable his friends and how violent his enemies, Paul might have been tempted to irreverence and blasphemy. Some have thought that these opponents were the thorn in the flesh. Their opposition sometimes seemed a stab in the back. Any one who has had to deal with cantankerous human nature as it sometimes manifests itself in the leadership of volunteer organizations will appreciate the feeling he must sometimes have had towards them.

John Wesley traveled four to five thousand miles a year on horseback, in search of opportunities to preach the Gospel. If Wesley had been happy at home, he might not have traveled so frequently nor gone so far. The question whether Paul was married has never been finally settled, but some think an unsympathetic wife was his "thorn"; others, supposing him not to have been married, affirm that sexual temptations were his constant harassment.

It seems better, however, to believe that Paul's thorn represented physical suffering. The possible nature of that suffering, too, has been widely construed. Among the last entries in Henry Martyn's journal is this: "Soon after sunset the ague came on again ... my fever increased to a violent degree; the heat in my eyes and forehead was so great that the fire almost made me frantic." Malarial fever can do that to a man, and its flaming temperatures are accompanied by headaches which make one feel that a torture stake is being driven through his brain. Malarial fever was a common affliction in the Roman world, and some suppose this was Paul's "thorn." Support for this argument is sought in Paul's visits to Galatia: he went into the highlands of that region to get the relief afforded by a less enervating climate than that of the Mediterranean coastlands. Galatians (4.13) says: "you know it was because of a bodily ailment that I preached the gospel to you at first."

Eye-trouble was also common in the ancient world, and

there are some who believe this was Paul's malady. We know from Acts (9.8f) that he was stricken blind on the Damascus road: "Saul arose from the ground; and when his eyes were opened, he could see nothing; so they led him by the hand and brought him into Damascus. And for three days he was without sight." Later, following a visit from Ananias, "something like scales fell from his eyes and he regained his sight" (Acts 9.18). The theory is that this left him with vision permanently impaired. Support for this view is sought in two passages in Galatians. Recalling experiences on his visit among them he says: "though my condition was a trial to you, you did not scorn or despise me, but received me as an angel of God, as Christ Jesus. What has become of the satisfaction you felt? For I bear you witness that, if possible, you would have plucked out your eyes and given them to me" (Gal. 4.14f).

What more calculated to make his presence among them a trial than secretion from diseased eyes? And the reference to plucking out eyes and handing them over—is that like our saying, "I'd cut off my right arm and give it to you"? Or does it literally mean that the most appropriate thing they could have done would be to replace his ailing eyes with their own? The other possible allusion to eye trouble is one which the King James Version misses entirely, with its rendering of Galatians (6.11): "Ye see how large a letter I have written unto you with mine own hand." This makes the passage refer to the length of the epistle, whereas the Greek plainly refers to the size of the characters. The REVISED STANDARD rightly translates: "See with what large letters I am writing to you with my own hand." Does this mean that ophthalmia required him to write in a giant scrawl if he were to make it out himself?

Others consider that epilepsy was his affliction, and the ambiguous Scriptural evidence they use supports that. By those who prefer picturesque speech to technical accuracy, epilepsy is sometimes referred to as "the falling sickness." En route to Damascus, says Dr. Luke, Paul "fell to the ground" (Acts 9.4). Prelude to the epileptic seizure is the aura, a premonitory symptom in which the patient has the sensation of light vapor rising from the limbs or body towards the head. The prelude to Paul's falling to the ground, as related in Acts (9.3), is that "suddenly a light from heaven flashed about him." Epileptic convulsions are not necessarily inconsistent with great mental and spiritual power, as is evidenced by some of history's great men who are said to have been epileptics: Julius Caesar, Peter the Great, King Alfred, Mohammed, Napoleon, Dostoevsky.

Galatians (4.14), "though my condition was a trial to you, you did not scorn me," has also been held applicable to one subject to attacks of epilepsy. Fierce headaches also characterize the paroxysms. Sir William Ramsay says: "Within my experience several persons, innocent of Pauline theorising, have described it as 'like a red-hot bar thrust through the forehead.'" It has been observed that if Paul's experience on the Damascus road was an epileptic convulsion, no other epileptic seizure in history has had quite such far-reaching results.

Various other afflictions have been suggested, at one time or another, as being Paul's malady: earache, toothache, migraine headache, bladder, kidney, or gall stones; hemorrhoids, leprosy, stammering. It is easy to understand how any one suffering any of these afflictions would think Paul must have had that. None of these, however, has much by way of Scriptural evidence that can be cited in support of the diagnosis. Still one other conjecture is that Paul's "thorn" referred to wounds remaining in his body from one of the stonings to which he was subjected in the course of his missionary journeys for example (Acts 14.5). At one point he was so severely injured by the infuriated mob that they "dragged him out of the city, supposing that he was dead" (Acts 14.19). Did this experience leave wounds that did not heal?

Paul was not only not spared pain but he regarded the pain which he had as a gracious warning from God: "to keep me from being too elated by the abundance of revelations, a thorn was given me in the flesh, a messenger of Satan, to harass me, to keep me from being too elated." In that sentence is summed up the whole mystery of pain. When it seems to limit and circumscribe, we deem it "a messenger of Satan." Yet in the context of our total experience we come to see it in a different light. Bodily affliction sometimes saves us from pride and domineering and self-confidence and boasting, in which case it is seen really to be a boon. "Though our outer nature is wasting away," says Paul (2 Cor. 4.16f), "our inner nature is being renewed every day. For this slight momentary affliction is preparing for us an eternal weight of glory beyond all comparison." It is not good to be unable to cry, and pain may be the gift of God. The Scripture describes a symbolic act by which others may lighten our pain by sharing it.

29. Anointing with Oil

There are philosophies which are concerned only to emphasize the "spiritual." In view of the close relationship now known to exist between body and spirit, it is important not to overlook the fact that, in the Scripture, "spiritual" values are often mediated through physical acts. The Fourth Gospel represents Jesus, his last night on earth, as taking a towel and washing the disciples' feet and when he had finished he said to them: "Do you know what I have done to you? You call me Teacher and Lord; and you are right, for so I am. If I then, your Lord and Teacher, have washed your feet, you also ought to wash one another's feet. For I have given you an example that you also should do as I have done to you" (John 13.12-15).

The little word "as" is the one most often emphasized by the commentators: we are to do *as* Christ did—not *what* Christ did. Jesus has here exemplified the spirit in which we are to act, and any deed of self-sacrificing humility, whether it be carried out in precisely this way or not, is held to be a fulfilment of our Lord's command "that you should also do as I have done." Moreover, it is customary to point out that the physical circumstances have changed. Jesus' specific act here presupposes dusty roads and sandaled feet. We seldom go on foot and when we do it is along a sidewalk. We wear shoes that really protect, and when we enter a home we do not take them off.

Since the circumstances of our time prevent us from doing what Jesus did, we must therefore discover ways of doing *as* he did. But what act of humility is there which is quite the equivalent of foot washing? I Timothy (5.10) sets forth the qualifications of every woman who would be enrolled for office in the early church: "she must be well attested for her good deeds, as one who has brought up children, shown hospitality, washed the feet of the saints, relieved the afflicted and devoted herself to doing good in every way." At many times and places in Christian history the foot washing ceremony has been carried out once a year.

The Latin word for commandment is *mandatum*—it has made its way into English as mandate. From *mandatum* is derived the term Maundy, applied to Thursday in Holy

Week. On this day our Lord gave a new command, and on this day His mandate must be obeyed. But how? In many parts of Christendom the command has been taken with literalness. Throughout the Middle Ages the ceremony was performed in European courts and monasteries. Kings, bishops, priests washed the feet of their inferiors. The Austrian emperor used to wash the feet of the twelve oldest poor men in Vienna, and British monarchs were accustomed to wash the feet of as many poor men as they were years old. A reminiscence of this survives still in England in the giving of Maundy alms, silver coins freshly minted and distributed to the poor.

Some church groups still practice foot washing and assure us that it is a soul-renewing experience in humility. One has to stoop in order to perform this rite, and menial service for another cannot be done with haughtiness. Neighbors who have quarreled cannot continue to hold a grudge if they submit themselves to this sacrament. A minister reports that feelings of hostility, engendered by lay opposition, invariably disappear when he washes the laymen's feet. Those who feel that the custom has been outmoded must be sure to find the moral equivalent of foot washing.

The Letter of James prescribes another physical act through which healing may be mediated. It contains specific provisions for treatment of illness by the church: "Is any among your sick? Let him call for the elders of the church, and let them pray over him, anointing him with oil in the name of the Lord; and the prayer of faith will save the sick man, and the Lord will raise him up" (James 5.14). The first element in this prescription is the willing co-operation of the patient. If he wishes to receive the help that may come from the believing fellowship, he must ask for it. "Let him call for the elders of the church." When people are ill, they send for the physician, but they somehow expect their church friends

to find out about it. A woman whose uncle died was much
incensed that her own pastor did not call. But he did not
hear of her grief until later. He then asked if she had summoned the undertaker. "Why certainly," she said. "Well,"
said the minister, "I should have appreciated your notifying
me, too."

Anointment with oil was used in ancient Israel for medicinal purposes. This is indicated by a passage in the book of
the prophet Isaiah in which the nation's sins are spoken of
as if they were a grievous illness:

> "Why will you still be smitten,
>   that you continue to rebel?
> The whole head is sick,
>   and the whole heart faint.
> From the sole of the foot even to
>   the head,
>   there is no soundness in it,
> but bruises and sores
>   and bleeding wounds;
> they are not pressed out, or bound
>   up
> or softened with oil" (Is. 1.5-6).

The Gospels represent the practice of anointing with oil as
having been carried out by the disciples when Jesus sent
them through the countryside. Mark (6.12f) gives this account of their mission: "So they went out and preached that
men should repent. And they cast out many demons, and
anointed with oil many that were sick and healed them."

Upon the basis of these Biblical passages the Roman
church has developed the sacrament of extreme unction,
defined as the "sacrament through which those in danger of
death from bodily illness or infirmity receive, by the anointing with holy oil and by the prayer of the priest, the grace
of God for their spiritual strength." The Council of Trent de-

clared "extreme unction to be a sacrament, instituted by Christ, conferring good, remitting sins, and comforting the infirm." Since the sacrament is concerned with the remission of sin, the organs of the body which may have been associated with sin are anointed.

The five senses are sight, hearing, smell, taste, and touch. Hence, lest one has sinned in any of these ways, the oil is applied to the eyes, the ears, the nostrils, the lips, and the hands. Since one may have sinned by walking astray or in the realm of sex, the feet and genitals (of men) are anointed. The anointing is accompanied by the prayer, "Through this holy unction and His own most tender mercy may the Lord pardon thee whatever sins or faults thou hast committed by sight, hearing, smell, taste, touch, walking, carnal delectation." In the Eastern Orthodox church the ointment is applied to the forehead, the chin, the cheeks, the hands, the nostrils, and the breast.

The manual of devotion in the Roman church says: "Our Lord and Saviour Jesus Christ, in His tender solicitude for those whom He has redeemed by His precious blood, has been pleased to institute another sacrament, to help us at that most important hour on which eternity depends—the hour of death. This sacrament is called Extreme Unction, or the last anointing." This would seem to be in error on at least two counts. At dangerous turns in the highway we are sometimes confronted with the sign "Where will you spend eternity?" The philosophy of the Roman church would seem to imply that the answer to that question depends at least in part upon whether we do or do not receive extreme unction. It is administered "at that most important hour on which eternity depends." It is the teaching of the Scripture, however, that the kind of life we have in "eternity" depends upon the kind of life which has been here begun. It hardly hinges upon what happens to us in *articulo mortis*.

The second point which seems to be ignored by the Roman philosophy is the obvious intent of the Biblical anointing. The Letter of James enjoins the anointing of the sick for the purpose of speeding his recovery: "The prayer of faith will save the sick man, and the Lord will raise him up" (James 5.15). In the Roman church, however, this anointing is not done if the patient is thought to have a chance of recovery. Since it is regarded as preparation for death, it is administered only to those who are thought to be on the threshold of dying. Anointing the sick with oil, accomplished in the fellowship of good people, is designed to restore the patient to his health. The anointing of one person by the other seems to be symbolic of the influences that pass from person to person and from life to life.

The anointing of the sick is an apostolic custom not much practiced now. Some churches have forms of worship providing for it. In the Book of Common Prayer of the Anglican Church there is "The Order for the Visitation of the Sick," to which is appended a brief addition called "Unction of the Sick." It is stated that "When any sick person shall in humble faith desire the ministry of healing through Anointing or Laying on of Hands, the minister may use such portions of the foregoing office as he shall think fit, and the following"— namely, a prayer that God will "drive away all pain of soul and body," and that the patient, "being restored to soundness of health" may offer to God "praise and thanksgiving," and the words: "I anoint with oil (or I lay my hand upon thee), in the Name of the Father, and of the Son, and of the Holy Ghost; beseeching the mercy of our Lord Jesus Christ, that all thy pain and sickness of body being put to flight, the blessing of health may be restored unto thee."

Upon the basis of this, a number of parishes of the Episcopal church have recently developed services of healing. "A Free Church Book of Common Prayer," issued by the non-Anglican churches of Britain, contains "A Form that may be used at the Healing of Infirm Persons," with a similar provision either for the laying on of hands or anointing with oil, and the prayer: "God give a blessing to this work: and grant that these sick persons, whom we have anointed, and upon whom, after the example of the holy apostles, we have laid our hands, may recover; through the mercy of Jesus Christ our Lord."

Those who have ministered to the dying know that, when everything else has ceased to move them, they will often respond to the words of the 23rd Psalm. In it is a passage which suggests that the church needs more and more to appreciate the influences for good that they may be transmitted through that use of oil which is called unction:

> "Thou anointest my head with oil,
>   my cup overflows.
> Surely goodness and mercy shall follow me
>   all the days of my life;
> and I shall dwell in the house of the Lord
>   for ever."

With this kind of confidence, rest and sleep may come quickly even amid circumstances of anxiety.

30. When You Lie Down

Americans like to think of this as the Engineering Age, but former President Dodds, of Princeton, insists that it is really the Phenobarbital Age. Before making his entrance, the actor takes a "blue angel" to induce a relaxed appearance. Before a difficult court case, the lawyer swallows a pink tablet to bolster his self-confidence. Before a meeting to arrange the big deal, the tense business man gulps a white capsule to ease his nerves. Before an examination, the student takes a yellow "goof ball" to help him breeze through. For some socially ambitious women, the sleeping pill is as much a bedtime necessity as the toothbrush.

Chemical extracts and compounds developed within the present decade appear to give patients a feeling of peace and contentment and freedom from anxiety. It is estimated that in a recent year three out of the ten compounds prescribed most frequently by physicians were tranquilizers. The American Psychiatric Association has warned that the use of these drugs as "medicines for the relief of every day tensions" is "medically unsound and constitutes a public danger."

Augustine held that all human perversity and vice consists either in using what we ought to enjoy or enjoying what we ought to use. So with the "happiness" drugs. Tranquilizers make it possible for more effective treatment to be administered to disturbed patients in mental hospitals, and are "useful adjuncts" in the treatment of psychiatric disorders in clinical and private practice. But the casual use of these drugs has for its end result something other than happiness. Barbiturates are desirable and effective in certain situations. They keep epilepsy under control; they relieve the agony of cancer sufferers; they are helpful in the urgencies of shock or sorrow. In all such cases they are administered under the direction of a physician and in carefully regulated quantities.

When we are not ill, life provides other ways of falling asleep. A brisk walk and hot bath at bedtime will often turn the trick. In addition, the Bible has much help for us here. Jesus described how "the cares of the world, and the delight in riches, and the desire for other things, enter in and choke the word" (Mark 4.19). The same vicious trio choke off sleep. The "cares of the world" involve not only the quest for this world's goods, but also concern to impress others with our prestige and importance. This leads to parties with extravagant use of food and drink which are anything but sleep-inducing. "Sweet is the sleep of a laborer," says Ecclesiastes (5.12), "whether he eats little or much; but the surfeit of the rich man will not let him sleep."

The "delight in riches" may also keep us awake. One of Jesus' sermons was interrupted by a covetous man's plea: "Teacher, bid my brother divide the inheritance with me" (Luke 12.13). Jesus replied with the story of the rich farmer who thought he could satisfy his soul with things. The good earth had been kind to him and he said to himself: "Soul, you have ample goods laid up for many years; take your ease, eat, drink, be merry" (Luke 12.19). It was in the midst of his carousing that God said: "Fool! This night your soul is required of you; and the things you have prepared, whose will they be?" (Luke 12.20).

Those whose one purpose it is to lay up treasure for themselves are never satisfied, but have their hearts always set on accumulating yet other things. In the 8th century B.C. there were grasping men in ancient Israel who could not take time out even for the sabbath rest and other religious observances. So greedy were they that they said:

"When will the new moon be over,
 that we may sell grain?
And the sabbath,
 that we may offer wheat for sale,
 that we may make the ephah small and the shekel great,
 and deal deceitfully with false balances,
 that we may buy the poor for silver
 and the needy for a pair of sandals?" (Amos 8.5f).

Hatred in our hearts is another thing that may keep us awake. Nebuchadnezzar, king of Babylon, was determined to make the Jews conform to his own practices with regard to food and drink and worship. Perturbed at their refusal, the king "had dreams; and his spirit was troubled, and his sleep left him" (Dan. 2.1). Trying to get rid of Daniel by throwing him to the lions did not make it any easier for him to rest. He spent that "night fasting; no diversions were brought to him, and sleep fled from him. Then, at break of day, the king arose and went in haste to the den of lions" (Dan. 6.18f), where he was delighted to find that the evil which he had plotted had not come to pass.

The men and women of the Bible could sleep in peace and quiet because their lives were under the direction and control of One who delighted to give to others the rest He never needs. Hagar's words, "Thou art a God of seeing" (Gen. 16.13) are ordinarily understood as referring to "the watchful eye of God's unceasing judgment." They here refer, however, to "the glad acknowledgment of the heavenly grace that beholds our human needs." Hagar knew what the Psalmist made plain:

"He who keeps you will not slumber,
  Behold, He who keeps Israel
  will neither slumber nor sleep" (Psalm 121.3, 4).

Psalm 4 is an evening prayer. Luther was so fond of its closing words that he desired them to be used as a requiem for him:

"In peace I will both lie down and sleep;
  for thou alone, O LORD, makest me dwell in safety."

Psalm 3 is a morning prayer; one who has known the refreshing sleep that comes from quiet trust in God could say:

"I lie down and sleep;
  I wake again, for the LORD sustains me."

Paul writes to the Philippians (4.7): "the peace of God, which passes all understanding, will keep your hearts and your minds in Christ Jesus." The verb there translated "keep" is a military term. It describes a garrison, standing watch over a city. God's peace is the garrison thrown round about the city of Mansoul, and with that kind of protection there is no need for us to stay awake! During the bombing attacks of the Second World War, Britishers spent many hours in subway stations and other underground retreats. In some air raid shelters a doctor posted placards bearing the words of Proverbs (3.24): "When you lie down, your sleep will be sweet." The Gospels picture Jesus calmly sleeping through a great storm at sea that frightened the hardened sailors. "And they went and woke Him, saying, 'Save, Lord; we are perishing.' And He said to them, 'Why are you afraid, O men of little faith?'" (Matthew 8.24ff).

Sir Wilfred Grenfell reports an incident in which his quiet confidence in the Eternal goodness enabled him to sleep calmly in the face of danger and threatened disaster. On Easter Sunday of 1908 he received a summons to go about 60 miles to the aid of a young man upon whom he had operated a fortnight before for acute bone disease of the thigh. He guessed that the leg would probably have to be amputated, and realized there was no time to lose. Accordingly, he set out on his komatik pulled by eight dogs. By cutting across the ice, instead of going all the way around the bay, he figured he could save several miles and much precious time. It was the 21st of April, and the ice had already begun to break up. The thaw was much farther along than he realized, and presently he found himself adrift on an ice pan, heading for the open sea.

Should the pan reach the open sea, it would melt and he would drown. The possibility of summoning aid seemed nil. The matches he had brought were soaked, so that there was no way to start a fire. Another man might have been driven into a frenzy, but he calmly prepared to make the best of the situation, resolving to do all he could to protect himself from the elements and not worry. He killed three of the dogs, later erecting in his home a plaque "To the Memory of Three Noble Dogs, Moody, Watch, Spy, Whose Lives Were Given for Mine on the Ice." From the skins of the animals he fashioned a bloody jacket to cut the wind and keep him from freezing. Their piled-up bodies also formed a protecting barrier. Disarticulating the legs of the dead animals, he managed by fastening them together to construct a rude flagpole from which floated his shirt, in the desperate hope of attracting the attention of some one on shore.

Having done all that he could, Sir Wilfred then lay down against the warm bodies of the dogs that remained, and fell asleep. "The rocking of my cradle on the waves," he says, "had helped me to sleep, and I felt as well as I ever did in my life ... I could not help laughing at my position, standing hour after hour waving my shirt at those barren and lonely cliffs; but I can honestly say that from first to last not a single sensation of fear crossed my mind." The sequel is that some had seen his frantic distress signals, and the next morning a boat, powerfully manned, pushed its way through the ice to rescue him.

The point here is that in the face of what seemed hopeless odds he retained a quiet confidence in God that enabled him to sleep normally and refreshingly. "My own faith in the mystery of immortality," he writes, "is so untroubled that it now seemed almost natural to be passing to the portal of death from an ice pan. Quite unbidden, the words of the old hymn kept running through my head:

> 'My God, my Father, while I stray
> Far from my home on life's rough way,
> Oh, help me from my heart to say,
> Thy will be done.' " *

---

* Cf. *Forty Years for Labrador*; Boston: Houghton Mifflin Co., 1932, Pp. 201-209.

People with that kind of religion may require sleeping pills after an operation, but have no need of them at any other time. The hours of rest may turn out to be a wondrous time of rejoicing.

31. Songs in the Night

So precious is sleep to man that the ancients regarded Hypnos, who survives in our English hypnosis, as a god. In the British Museum there is a bronze head of this ethnic deity. Socrates held that the dreams of a good man are pure and prophetic, because in sleep the noblest elements of the soul are free to lead a life unfettered by the demands of the body. The Bible knows only one God. All is from Him. Sleep is one of His gifts to mankind. This is one of the ways in which God speaks:

> "In a dream, in a vision of the night,
>   when deep sleep falls upon men,
>   while they slumber on their beds,
> then he opens the ears of men,
>   and terrifies them with warnings,
> that he may turn man aside from his deed,
>   and cut off pride from man" (Job 33.15-17).

The refreshing and well-earned sleep of the toiler is contrasted in the Bible with the excessive and debilitating sleep of the slothful who sleep on simply because they are too lazy to get up:

"How long will you lie there, O sluggard?
    When will you arise from your sleep?
A little sleep, a little slumber,
    A little folding of the hands to rest,
and poverty will come upon you like a vagabond,
    and want like an armed man" (Prov. 6.9f cf. 20.13; 24.33f).

A Confession of Faith dating from Reformation times inter-
prets the commandment against murder to mean among
other things, that one ought not to sleep too much. To sleep
one's life away is in a sense to destroy one's life. Proverbs
(10.5) has this warning for adolescents:

"A son who gathers in summer is prudent,
    but a son who sleeps in harvest brings shame."

Overwork may lead to sleeplessness. For twenty years
Jacob toiled for his uncle Laban: "I served you fourteen
years for your two daughters, and six years for your flock,
and you have changed my wages ten times" (Gen. 31.41).
Long and strenuous days were followed by long and sleepless nights: "by day the heat consumed me," he says (Gen.
31.40), "and the cold by night, and my sleep fled from my
eyes."

On the other hand, a normal work load will enable one to
know the joyous alternation of labor and rest. "The kingdom
of God," said Jesus (Mark 4.26, 27), "is as if a man should
scatter seed upon the ground, and should sleep and rise night
and day, and the seed should sprout and grow, he knows not
how." The farmer is responsible only for faithfulness in plow-
ing and planting. He does not have to lie awake all night
worrying about whether the seed will grow!

Psalm 127.2 reminds us of how futile it is to try to do for
ourselves what only God can do for us:

"It is vain that you rise up early,
  to go late to rest,
   eating the bread of anxious toil;
     for he gives to his beloved in sleep."

Men go to work earlier than usual, spend a long day in office
or store or factory, return at night to eat an unsatisfying
dinner—all this in order to provide what they call security
for their families. There is a better security, though—the quiet
confidence in a God "whose goodness faileth never."

There is a German proverb, "God bestows His gifts during
the night." The hurried business man, anxious to bring home
another dollar, may be robbing his loved ones of the security
they really want, the untroubled affection of a father not too
tired to enter into family fun. Earlier translations made this
verse read: "It is vain for you to rise up early, to sit up late,
to eat the bread of sorrows; for so he giveth his beloved
sleep." This hardly accords with our human experiences. The
man who spends long days in anxious toil is precisely the
one to whom God does not give sleep.

The REVISED STANDARD VERSION correctly renders: "for he
gives to his beloved in sleep." A normal day's work is one
of the ways in which God provides for us; that may make us
comfortably tired, so that we fall asleep readily. But sleep,
too, comes "direct from Heaven's bounty"—and anxious toil
will rob us of that. In sleep God gives to us many things: forgetfulness of the wrongs we have suffered, strength for un-
finished tasks, zest for a new day. Because a part of the mind
seems always active, God sometimes gives us in sleep the
solutions to our problems. The name that eluded us during
the day is in the forefront of the mind when we awake. The
key to the mathematical puzzle which baffled is suddenly
obvious.

In sleep also God banishes our discouragement. Elijah

had triumphed over the hosts of Baal, but Jezebel still sought to destroy the prophet. Feeling that life was no longer worth living, "he lay down and slept under a broom tree" (I Kings 19.5). While he slept, "an angel touched him, and said to him, 'Arise and eat'. . . And he arose and ate and drank, and went in the strength of that food forty days and forty nights" (I Kings 19.5, 8).

Sometimes sleep does not come. Moses, picturing a time of trouble for his people, described their anxiety: "Night and day you shall be in dread, and have no assurance of your life. In the morning you shall say, 'Would it were evening!' and at evening you shall say, 'Would it were morning!'" (Deut. 28.66f). Those for whom this is a description of personal experience will exclaim with the Psalmist (130.6):

"My soul waits for the Lord
     more than watchmen for the morning."

Physiologically, one of the functions of sleep is to give the heart a rest. Breathing is deep, the pulse is slowed, the muscles are relaxed. A generous proportion of these benefits —some estimate it as high as 85 per cent—will accrue to us whether we lose consciousness or not. There is, therefore, a real sense in which it does not matter whether we sleep. The important thing is to take the weight off our feet and relieve the heart of having to pump the blood uphill. Remembering this, we may cease to worry about dropping off to sleep, and thus put ourselves in the position of the man who said that whenever he had insomnia he went to bed and slept it off.

Since we do not need to worry about whether we sleep, we can put to good advantage the hours of waking. Psalm 4.4 says:

"Commune with your own hearts on your beds,
     and be silent."

The quiet darkness, with its lack of clamor and interruption, may bring calmer and wiser thoughts. One who is happily married reports that when sleep tarries he does not fret, but simply brings consciously to mind how good God has been to him in his family. He recalls the day he met the girl who became his wife, the merry times they had when the children were young, the richer blessings that now come through children happily grown to maturity.

Thoughts such as these crowd out the harassments of the world which keep sleep away—and with such delights one does not care whether sleep comes or not!

If sleep is prevented by illness, there are yet other uses for the hours of waking.

A writer tells us: "I remember learning gradually, when I could not sleep at night because of pain or discomfort, to pray not for myself but for all those, who, all over the world, were unable to sleep. This helps me to avoid tension and self-pity." In the First Letter of Peter, written to believers who were undergoing persecution, Christians are reminded of the way in which suffering may enlarge their sympathies. The temptation to wrong-doing and rebellion they are to resist, "knowing that the same experience of suffering is required of your brotherhood throughout the world" (I Peter 5.9).

In the book of Job, Elihu speaks of "God my Maker, who gives songs in the night" (Job 35.10). The Acts of the Apostles records that in Philippi Paul and Silas were remanded to jail for preaching a Gospel that disturbed the peace. In order to make sure they did not get away, the jailer "put them into the inner prison and fastened their feet in the stocks." This was not a very comfortable way to spend the night, and the historian tells us how they put in the hours: "about midnight Paul and Silas were praying and singing hymns to God" (Acts 16.25).

The Psalmist felt that nighttime opportunities to think about God and His greatness were among earth's finest joys:

"I commune with my heart in the night;
        I meditate and search my spirit" (Psalm 77.6).

"My soul is feasted as with marrow and fat,
        and my mouth praises thee with joyful lips,
When I think of thee upon my bed,
    and meditate on thee in the watches of the night" (Psalm 63.5f).

Upton Sinclair, most of whose books have sprung from an ardent desire for social and industrial reform, tells us that in his hurried life he has found a formula that will invoke sleep. Do not think about sleep at all, he advises, but say to yourself words such as these:

"God enfolds me, God surrounds me. God covers me with a living blanket. That blanket has power to drive away all other thoughts. It protects me and keeps me safe. Under its shelter God and I are alone. God watches over me, God helps me, God heals me. God teaches me. God guides me. God gives me peace—"

"And so on," he continues. "It doesn't matter which of the things you say. It doesn't matter how many times you repeat any of them. The point is that you keep your mind full of images and ideas of a power greater than yourself, a power which has the necessary strength, the necessary knowledge, to take care of you and do for you what you need." (*What God Means to Me*, New York: Farrar and Rinehart, 1936; p. 76.)

For the Christian there is a Presence even more personal. Paul in 1 Thessalonians (5.10) tells us that Christ "died for us so that whether we wake or sleep we might live with him." It is God in Christ whose radiance can make luminous the dark watches of the night. After six years of slavery in the north of Ireland, a young Scotsman of the fifth century was set free to return to his homeland. But whether waking or sleeping he was haunted by the remembrance of the country of his captivity. In a vision of the night there came to him a summons from across the western sea: "We entreat thee, holy youth, to come and walk with us." Like Paul before him, Patrick would not be "disobedient to the heavenly vision" (Acts 26.19). For more than thirty years he preached the gospel to his former captors.

Wherever he went, there was a hymn which St. Patrick chanted. For all who cannot sleep it can be an inspiring song in the night:

> Christ with me, Christ before me,
> Christ behind me, Christ in me,
> Christ below me, Christ above me,
> Christ at my right, Christ at my left,
> Christ in breadth, Christ in length,
> Christ in height.
> Christ in the heart of every one who thinks of me,
> Christ in the mouth of every one who speaks of me,
> Christ in the eye that sees me,
> Christ in the ear that hears me.

He who can chant this song will come "to know the love of Christ which surpasses knowledge" (Eph. 3.19).

32. Love Casts Out Fear

An elderly gentleman offered school children a prize for the best composition on "How to Overcome Habit." The winning essay read:

> "Habit is hard to overcome. If you take off the first letter, it doesn't change a bit. Take off another letter, and still you have a bit left. Take off another letter, and the whole of it remains. If you take off another, it is still not all used up. All of which goes to show that if you want to get rid of a habit, you must throw it off altogether."

But even this is not sufficient. Getting rid of bad habits is not a matter of throwing them off but rather of replacing them by something better. Fear and anger cannot be put off by degrees. It is the teaching of the Bible that many of the things which bring torment and disease to the body can be overcome by love. Love, says 1 Peter (4.8), "covers a multitude of sins." This is the New Testament version of Proverbs (10.12):

> "Hatred stirs up strife,
> but love covers all offenses."

It is not simply that the possession of this grace makes up for many other shortcomings and inadequacies, but rather that love draws a veil over the wrongs which others have done. This it does not do to condone the wrong, not to hush it up, not to conceal it from the authorities, but rather to keep it from damaging the spirits of those against whom it has been committed. To "cover" in the Bible often means to forgive. The American Indians speak of burying the hatchet, and the men of the Bible indicate that we can best get rid of an offense by drawing something over it. Enmity keeps on raking up old grudges; love consigns to oblivion the hurt done to it. This, too, has become proverbial wisdom among the Hebrews:

"He who forgives an offense seeks love,
 but he who repeats a matter alienates a friend" (Prov. 17.9)

When others have done us wrong, love quietly draws a veil over the scene. Within ourselves anger and fear are overcome, not by wishing, not by repeating some glib formula, but by "the expulsive power of a new affection." We cannot run away from fear: it will get there before us. We cannot subdue it, for it will be master in whatever house it inhabits. We cannot get rid of it simply by saying, "Begone!" Concentrating our attention upon it may serve only to intensify it. The only way to get the better of fear is to fill up our lives with something that will crowd it out. "There is no fear in love," says 1 John (4.18), "but perfect love casts out fear."

This is valid in every area of life. It is true of all three kinds of love. Our English language at this point is so poor that the one word "love" must do for experiences described by three different Greek words. First there is romantic love. This is the only form of love which Hollywood knows, and what Hollywood portrays oftentimes is not genuine love at all, but some perversion or prostitution of it. Romantic love has power to cast out fear. A shy, shrinking timorous girl suddenly becomes an effective person, filled with poise and charm. You ask the reason? She has fallen in love.

A lad, timid, awkward, frightened, overnight becomes self-reliant, resourceful, able always to put his best foot forward. What has happened? He has found the right girl, the only girl for him. Following the Second World War the large number of married students posed a serious problem for college administrators. The problem was largely a housing problem, however, rather than an academic one. Married students have been found winning more than their share of prizes and other academic distinctions. Of the 33 Phi Beta Kappas who graduated from Barnard College in a recent year, 14 were already married. "There's nothing to worry about on the emotional side after you're married," one of them explained, "so I did better work at college."

The distinctive Greek word for romantic love does not occur in the Bible, and romantic love as we know it was largely unknown in the ancient world. Yet in the Old Testament we have pictures of it. Laban required Jacob to work for him a long time before he would give him his daughter in marriage. "So Jacob served seven years for Rachel, and they seemed to him but a few days because of the love he had for her" (Gen. 29.20).

It was romantic love which brought both Robert Browning and Elizabeth Barrett Browning to the height of their literary achievements. "I, who . . . was caught up into love," sings Mrs. Browning, was "taught the whole of life in a new rhythm." But these words do not compare in power with those of Solomon's Song (8.7):

> "Many waters cannot quench love,
>   neither can floods drown it.
> If a man offered for love
>   all the wealth of his house,
>   it would be utterly scorned."

The second form of love is that normal human affection we have for those bound to us by ties of kinship. Folliott S. Pierpont felt that a joyous element ought to be introduced into the solemn service of communion, and domestic affec-

tion is one of the things he celebrates in a "Hymn of Grateful
Praise" which he wrote:

> "For the love which from our birth
> Over and around us lies
>
> .   .   .   .
>
> For the joy of human love,
> Brother, sister, parent, child."

Tension and strife sometimes arise between the members
of a family. If we grimly resolve to live with these, they may
lead to a breakdown in health. Here again love draws its
veil. Here again love pushes out hostility. Jacob and Esau
had had a falling-out. When Jacob heard that Esau and all
his retinue were drawing near, he "was greatly afraid and
distressed" (Gen. 32.7). Instead, however, of preparing an
ambush for his estranged brother, he sought to win him over.
Gift after gift he sent. These melted Esau's hard heart; although he refused to accept the gifts, he did respond to the
friendly overture, and when the brothers met, Jacob exclaimed, "truly to see your face is like seeing the face of God"
(Gen. 33.10).

This is what Paul means by "Do not be overcome by evil,
but overcome evil with good" (Rom. 12.21). The Gospels
indicate that the brothers of Jesus did not understand Him,
nor company with Him in the days of His public ministry.
They apparently thought that what their brother needed to
do was to give up his itinerant preaching and settle down to
help with the carpenter's business. There is special point,
therefore, in Paul's list of the resurrection appearances: "Then
he appeared to James" (1 Cor. 15.7). If James had misunderstood us, we might have thought that the best thing to do
was to leave him alone. But Jesus, drawing a veil across this
hardness of heart, "appeared to James," and this gracious

act of forgiveness made a great church leader out of his brother.

Love, in the distinctively Christian sense, means a wise and active desire for the well-being of others. The way to banish fear from our own lives is to become so absorbed in promoting the welfare of others as that concern about self will be forgotten. This is the way to peace and poise and good health. What Christianity means in this respect is sometimes made clear on the mission field. A student of the world scene tells us that one of the supreme tests of a religion is the attitude of its devotees in the face of an epidemic.

He had opportunity to observe how Christians behaved in an epidemic of cholera, a disease that strikes suddenly and is accompanied by high mortality. His verdict is that "nothing is more certain than this—that in cholera time the outcaste Christians stand ready when their neighbors, by their very panic, are creating conditions favorable to the spread of the disease; that they meet the disease, when it does come to them, with the courage born of Christian faith, and that some of them, especially those who have become teachers, often show magnificent courage and self-sacrifice in ministering to the sufferers both heathen and Christian."

Godfrey Phillips, in his book, *The Outcastes' Hope*, tells how on one occasion a pariah Christian who had become a catechist came into Secunderabad for cholera medicine. Just after he had reached the mission station, he learned that his own son, in the boys' home there, had been attacked by the disease. To the surprise and disappointment of the missionary, the catechist hurried off at once. The missionary learned later, what the catechist was surprised he did not guess from the first, that, confidently leaving his own son in the care of the missionary, the man had hurried off to help the villagers for whom he felt a sense of responsibility. There is a concern for others' troubles which results in forgetfulness of our own!

No wonder Paul says: "Make love your aim" (1 Cor. 14.1). The 13th chapter of 1 Corinthians is the classical description of what love is and does. We are sometimes told that Paul pays little attention to the earthly life of Christ. But this is his summary of that life. Each time the word "love" occurs, read instead "Jesus," and it will become clear that this chapter is a biography. Then read the same chapter, replacing the word "love" each time with your own name. Then you will learn what Christ meant when He said: "A new commandment I give to you, that you love one another; even as I have loved you, that you also love one another" (John 13.34). This kind of love will help us in many other relationships of life.

33. *Fear Not, nor Be Afraid*

The first play ever written specifically for radio was Archibald MacLeish's *The Fall of the City*. An unnamed community had been thrown into turmoil by a woman, known to be dead, who appeared for three days at the door of her tomb. At noon on the fourth day she spoke a riddle: "The city of masterless men will take a master. There will be shouting then, blood after." While the crowd is milling about, pondering her words, a messenger staggers in to announce that the Conqueror has landed from overseas.

Orators then step forward with various programs to propose: A pacifist counsels non-resistance; priests urge a return to the old gods; a general summons men to defend their city and die as freemen. Meanwhile, the Conqueror is drawing ever nearer. Huge in his armor, he marches into the central plaza and surveys the cowed populace, already kneeling before him. Then he opens his visor:

> "There's no one at all!
> No one! ...
> The helmet is hollow!
> The metal is empty! The armor is empty!"

The city has fallen before a figment of the popular imagination. MacLeish wrote his play as a commentary upon our times: "The people invent their oppressors; they wish to believe in them." It is a parable, too, of what happens in individual life. In the Bible, powerful expression of this truth is put into the mouth of Job (3.25):

> "For the thing that I fear comes upon me,
> and what I dread befalls me."

One has known a few people who were very much afraid of dogs. Why were they the ones dogs were always molesting? The answer seems to be that fear releases chemical substances in the body which give off an odor that is irritating to dogs. Fear creates the thing it is afraid of!

Those familiar with the life of the jungle tell us that man's impression of the ferocity of wild animals is greatly exaggerated. If surprised by some unexpected approach, most animals will turn to flight. Where they have attacked men, it is usually either because they themselves have been first attacked or because they have already become criminals among their own kind. After many years of studying wild animals, Grace Thompson Seton came to the conclusion that they were about 95 per cent safe. The prophet (Is. 11.8f) heard God say:

> "The sucking child shall play over the hole of the asp,
> and the weaned child shall put his hand on the adder's den.
> They shall not hurt or destroy
> in all my holy mountain."

During the Second World War, elephants in Burma trampled people in the villages—but this was because the "wild" beasts had been driven mad by the bombings which "Christian" men had inflicted upon their region.

That which people dread goes on happening to them, and fear is often responsible for infirmities of the body. In leaflets describing infantile paralysis, one paragraph, headed: "Remember, Facts Fight Fears," gives this advice to parents: "Don't let your anxiety or fear reach your children. A happy state of mind helps to obtain fuller recovery. Your own confidence will make things easier for you and for others."

Thirty-five years ago there was a small-town family afraid the children would catch this disease or that. Whenever chicken-pox or measles or mumps or influenza was known to be anywhere in the community, the children were not allowed to go to Sunday School lest they pick up the disease. In the same block lived a family whose children continued year after year to get medals for perfect attendance at Sunday School. The simple fact was that the first family caught practically every disease that came to town, the other seldom had sickness.

Legend tells of how an Eastern pilgrim encountered the Plague one day. "Where are you going?" asked the Pilgrim. "To Bagdad," was the reply, "to kill five thousand people." A few days later the same Pilgrim met the Plague again. "You told me you were going to Bagdad to kill five thousand people," complained the Pilgrim, "but instead you killed fifty thousand." "No," said the Plague, "I killed only five thousand, as I told you; the others died of fright."

The New Testament announces from the outset that Christ's coming was intended to banish fear. When Jesus was born, the message of the angels was: "Be not afraid" (Luke 2.10). At the tomb of the risen Savior the angelic message was the same: "Do not be afraid" (Mt. 28.5; cf.

Jesus' own word, verse 10). And ever in between, Jesus' ministry was given over to the banishment of fear. Men were afraid of tyrants and the evil powers of this world; Jesus said: "Do not fear those who kill the body but cannot kill the soul" (Mt. 10.28). The disciples felt that they were a helpless minority in a hostile world; Jesus said: "Fear not, little flock, for it is your Father's good pleasure to give you the kingdom" (Luke 12.32). The Apostles carried on this campaign for the banishment of fear: "For God did not give us a spirit of timidity," says the author of 2 Timothy (1.7), "but a spirit of power and love and self-control."

Ever since then, Christ has been helping men and women overcome fear. Among primitive peoples, the sacredness of certain persons and objects is symbolized by the Polynesian word taboo, implying that contact with these persons and objects is fraught with unknown danger. If an animal or bird is thought to be the protector of a tribe, then the huntsman must never kill or eat any of that species. On the Indonesian Island of Timor, crops and orchards and houses are protected by this device. It is said that "A palm branch stuck across an open door, showing that the house is tabooed, is a more effectual guard against robbery than any amount of locks and bars." Albert Schweitzer sometimes adapts this primitive belief to higher ends, as when he says to a new mother: "Your child's taboo is that he shall not touch alcohol."

Among the ancient Hebrews, the Ark of the testimony was symbolic of God's presence. Careful regulations were set forth for moving the Ark, in order that it might accompany the people on their journeys. One rule was that the bearers "must not touch the holy things, lest they die" (Num. 4.15). The priests were forbidden to "go in to look upon the holy things even for a moment, lest they die" (Num. 4.20). In 2 Sam. (6.3-8) and 1 Chron. (13.7-11) there is the strange story of Uzzah, who inadvertently touched the Ark and was stricken dead.

It is difficult to know exactly what the old writers are trying to tell us here. Due to mistakes made by copyists, the Hebrew text is obscure. There is some reason to believe that the original related how Uzzah slipped on animal droppings and struck his head on the stone of the threshing floor. Missionaries, however, tell of having seen strong men die of fright after they have inadvertently broken their taboo. It is interesting to speculate whether some such circumstance may lie back of the sudden deaths of Ananias and Sapphira, described in Acts (5.1-10).

In any case, the Old Testament writers give the impression that Uzzah dropped dead when he touched what was thought to be God's dwelling place. In the New Testament, however, God's dwelling place is not in a box but in human hearts and —supremely—in the person of One who was His Son. Men were afraid to come near the Ark, but they were not afraid to come near Jesus. This is strikingly emphasized in 1 John (1.1-3) where the author writes of the boldness with which men had approached Christ: "That which ... we have looked upon and touched with our hands ... we proclaim also to you."

So far as effect upon the body is concerned, fear and anger are quite alike. Both step up the heartbeat, increase the rate of breathing, release adrenaline into the system. Both prepare us for something. They differ in that for which they make ready. Anger prepares us to stand up and fight. Fear makes us want to run away and escape. On the lowest level this may be accomplished by the central nervous system without any conscious participation on our part. Prick your finger—or touch a radiator, and the threatened member is involuntarily drawn to safety. So the Scripture suggests that there are evils which we should dread and from which we should instinctively draw back. Among these are strong drink (Provs. 20.1; 23.29-35), the harlot (Provs. 6.23-29; 23.27f), and "the way of evil men" (Psalm 1; Provs. 4.14; 1.10).

There is a fear from which religion does not deliver us but under whose spell it puts us: "The fear of the Lord," says Proverbs (9.10), "is the beginning of wisdom." This, however, does not refer to fear in the sense of "painful emotion caused by a sense of impending danger," but rather to something which is entirely worthy and foundational for love. Wholesome respect for the Deity is the starting point of the life of confidence and trust. In Ecclesiasticus it is described thus:

"The fear of the Lord is glory and exultation,
    and gladness and a crown of rejoicing.
The fear of the Lord delights the heart,
    and gives gladness and joy and long life."

Fear of God will deliver a man from all other fears. It will deliver him from fear of enemies, because "If God is for us, who is against us?" (Rom. 8.31). It will deliver him from fear of what other people will say about him, since "man looks on the outward appearance, but the LORD looks on the heart" (1 Sam. 16.7). It will deliver him from fear that he cannot do his work well, for "I can do all things in Him who strengthens me" (Phil. 4.13). It will deliver him even from fear of death, since it puts all things in true perspective: "If we live, we live to the Lord, and if we die, we die to the Lord; so then, whether we live or whether we die, we are the Lord's" (Rom. 14.8). This helps us to see God's Providence in a new light.

34. God Works in Everything

Elton Trueblood, who was then director of religious information for the Voice of America, addressed a meeting of the National Council of Churches on the theme, "The Gospel We Communicate." He said that from where he sat it appeared that a five-fold emphasis was urgent: that God is the Creator of all that is; that, in Jesus, God became flesh; that every man's work is a Christian vocation; that Jesus came not simply to bring peace but also disturbance, a sword; that Jesus' service combines both sorrow and joy. Trueblood's wife, who had been at death's door for several weeks, had died the day before this address.

It was generally assumed that the engagement would be canceled, but Trueblood insisted on going through with it. There was tension throughout the assembly when he began to speak. About midway in the address he said: "If I had to give up all the Bible except a single verse, the one I would want to keep would be Romans (8.28): 'We know that in everything God works for good with those who love him, who are called according to his purpose.'" This is the REVISED STANDARD VERSION. The King James Bible at this point says something rather different: "And we know that all things work together for good, to them who are the called according to *his* purpose."

This is a passage often quoted glibly in time of sorrow. It is especially apt to be used by younger ministers. Older men know that for grief that is new and deep there are no words, and that it is better to say nothing than to be overfacile. One who stands by loyally does not need to open his mouth to let the bereaved know of his sympathy. Those who think they must say something, however, quote Romans (8.28): "And we know that all things work together for good to them that love God, to them who are the called according to his purpose."

Grief-stricken men and women sometimes quote it to themselves. One has heard it repeated by parents whose 16-year-old son met death by accident, and by a mother and father whose daughter had committed suicide, taking with her her infant child. However hard it may be to believe, since it is in the Bible they thought it must be accepted unquestioningly. Not all have been so docile. One woman who had been widowed quite early in life said that she was sure that in her case it was not true.

She asked herself the reason. "We know that all things work together for good to them that love God." Outsiders might say it was because she did not love God, but she honestly and earnestly believed that she did love God. "—to them who are the called according to *his* purpose"—she then decided that the reason that in her case all things had not worked together for good was that she was not among the called according to His purpose—but there was small comfort in that.

A minister tried to explain that there is a certain emphasis on togetherness in the text. It is not said that all things separately work for good, but only that "all things work together for good." Individual circumstances may seem against us, but it is when things are seen in their totality that the beneficent purpose shines out. Ink spilled on a handkerchief seemed to ruin it, but the artist concealed the ink spot in a beautiful pattern that greatly enhanced the worth of the handkerchief.

The story is told of a clergyman who found even this hard to believe. At the age of 68 he said that he had never had a doubt, but within a year an experience had befallen of which he wrote: "In that dark hour I became almost an atheist. For God had set his foot upon my prayers and treated my petitions with contempt. If I had seen a dog in such agony as mine, I would have pitied and helped the dumb beast; yet God spat upon me and cast me out as an offense—out into the waste wilderness and the night black and starless." It was the death of his wife which caused such overwhelming emotion. No use telling a man in that mood that "all things work together for good."

One clergyman went so far as to assure his people that "Even the sins of believers work for their good." When this did not seem very convincing he went on to say: "It is not sin in itself that works the good, but God who overrules its effects to his children,—shows them, by means of it, what is in their hearts, as well as their entire dependence on himself, and the necessity of walking with him more closely." This is a comforting doctrine that readily passes over into acquiescence in sin on account of the great good which an overruling God may bring out of it. Paul himself explicitly rejects this contention in the same letter to Romans: "where sin increased, grace abounded all the more ... What shall we say then? Are we to continue in sin that grace may abound? By no means!" (Rom. 5.20; 6.1f).

The teacher of an adult Bible class, a man then in his seventies, reported that every time the lesson text across the years had included this verse he had been compelled to inform his class that he did not believe it. He was sure that somehow there must have been an error in transmission. He was convinced that no inspired writer could ever have said a thing like that. It was his own experience which had led him to this conviction. His father, a Methodist minister, had died when he, a boy of twelve, was the oldest of five children. The widowed mother had no financial resources, and society in those days had not gotten around to making provision at all for such a situation.

The oldest son had dreamed of emulating his father and going into the ministry, but had instead to drop out of school and go to work at once. There was never an opportunity to get the education he wanted. In spite of the financial contributions he made to the home, his mother and her brood continued to have a desperately hard time. He could not see that these circumstances had worked together for anybody's good. There it was, written in the Bible, but he did not believe it. An error must have occurred somewhere.

It was therefore with a tremendous sense of relief that he discovered the reading in the REVISED STANDARD VERSION: "We know that in everything God works for good with those who love him, who are called according to his purpose." This rests upon a more ancient Greek text, and is evidently what Paul wrote in the beginning.

It is not said that things work together at all. Things really are neutral, with no power to work either good or bad. The word "circumstances" simply means "things that stand around," and circumstances cannot of themselves affect us one way or the other—it depends upon what we make of the circumstances or what we let them do to us. It is said that, no matter how desperate our plight, God can still do something with us and for us: "in everything God works for good."

That "all things work together for good" may sometimes appear preposterous, at others it may seem merely platitudinous. But this is revelation! No circumstances may overtake us but that in them God may work out something to our advantage. If the statement merely were that "all things work together for good," then there would be no need for morality. If everything is going to turn out for the best anyway, then why not take the shortest way with your enemies? Why not live for show? Why not devote yourself to the accumulation of things? But difficult circumstances appear in a different light if we are aware that even in them God may work for good.

This means that adversities need not overwhelm us, but God can deliver us from them all. At the time David became king he remembered how this had been many times demonstrated in his own experience and spoke gratefully of God "who has redeemed my life out of every adversity" (2 Sam. 4.9). In one of the Psalms attributed to him we read:

"I will rejoice and be glad for thy steadfast love,
    because thou has seen my affliction,
        thou hast taken heed of my adversities,
    and hast not delivered me into the hand of the enemy;
    thou hast set my feet in a broad place"
                                        (Psalm 31.7f).

This does not give any glib solution to the ultimate problem of evil, yet it may indicate that in hardship and adversity there are meanings of which we have not always been aware. The cynical author of Ecclesiastes puts it this way: "In the day of prosperity be joyful, and in the day of adversity consider; God has made the one as well as the other." In adversity there is opportunity to consider, and one of the things God sometimes then does for us is to teach us the way we should have taken. The author of Psalm 119 (67) records that it was in this fashion God dealt with him:

"Before I was afflicted I went astray;
    but now I keep thy word.
Thou art good and doest good;
    teach me thy statutes."

Many another Bible biography could be cited as illustration of all this. Joseph was sold into slavery, unjustly accused by a designing woman, and cast into prison. Neither individually nor collectively did these evil circumstances work for

good. But in these evil circumstances God was working for
good, so that Joseph eventually could say to his brothers, "As
for you, you meant evil against me; but God meant it for
good" (Gen. 50.20).

What is true of the Bible can be traced also in history.
Matthew Fontaine Maury was a young seaman with pros-
pects and hopes of a brilliant career as a naval officer. At the
age of 33 he was crippled in a stagecoach accident: he had
given his seat to a lady and was the only victim of the over-
turn. His career at sea was ended. Much to his disgust he
was confined to a desk in a landlocked harbor. But from this
desk he worked out the principles of direction and velocity
for wind and wave. The weather charts and forecasts, upon
which much of present-day life depends, were made possible
by Maury's discoveries and calculations. There is not a ship
that sails the sea but uses his principles of navigation.

At a dark moment in Israel's history, a messenger of God
appeared to the despondent leader, Gideon. "The LORD is
with you," said the messenger (Judg. 6.12f), "you mighty man
of valor," and Gideon said to him, "Pray, sir, if the LORD is
with us, why then has all this befallen us?"

Gideon's question is that of many a perplexed and disap-
pointed soul: If God is with us, why did this loss, this sorrow,
this tragedy happen to me? The answer certainly does not
lie in any facile assurance that if we just keep our chin up
everything is bound to turn out all right. Before Jesus came,
no real answer was possible. Many evil forces conspired to
bring about his death, but in that tragedy God was working
for good. Thus it was that Paul interpreted his own frustra-
tions and defeats. He writes from prison: "I want you to
know, brethren, that what has happened to me has really
served to advance the gospel" (Phil. 1.12). Awareness that
God deals thus with us in every time of trouble may make
us sensitive to the situation and needs of others.

35. Love Draws a Veil

The Cunard steamship company has had a long tradition of giving its vessels names ending in "–ia": Berengaria, Mauretania, Carpathia, Caledonia. When the company was about to complete the first of the two large liners built in the years between wars, the decision had been made to call it "Victoria." Discussing the matter with King George V, the chairman of the board said: "Your Majesty, we have decided to name the vessel after one of Britain's most noble queens." "Oh," said the king, "Her Majesty will be pleased." And so it was that the great ship came to be called "Queen Mary." The queen herself died without ever having learned how the vessel got its name. She supposed that from the beginning the company's intention had been to honor her.

Here was a case where officials in the realm of trade and commerce did not wish to give offense either to the king or the queen, and the monarch's hurried and tactless assumption was quietly smoothed over without rebuke or hurt. No moral principle was at stake here, and the governors of the Cunard company felt it better to change their plans than to humiliate royalty. Not many individuals in our world will ever be confronted with that kind of situation, but the Scripture does urge upon us a constant willingness to cover up the failures and shortcomings, not of ourselves, but of others. "Above all," says 1 Peter (4.8), "hold unfailing your love for one another, since love covers a multitude of sins."

Here is the obligation that rests upon each human being to help others maintain a life of health and wholeness. The King James Version at this point reads: "And above all things

211

have fervent charity among yourselves: for charity shall cover the multitude of sins." This is one of several passages where the earliest English tradition, "Love," has been restored by the REVISED STANDARD VERSION. The Greek term here is the distinctive Christian word for love, and it was uniformly so translated by Tyndale, the Great Bible, and the Bishops' Bible. In the second edition of the Bishops' Bible, published in 1572, there were 32 instances where "love" was replaced by "charity."

The latter term did not mean "charity" in the limited modern sense of relieving the needs of the poor. It was simply an Anglicizing of the word *caritas,* found in the Latin Bible. *Caritas,* derived from the adjective meaning "dear," describes love other than romantic love (for which the Latin has the special term *amor*). Of the 112 New Testament occurrences of the Greek noun meaning a wise and active desire for the well-meaning of others, in 32 instances "love" was replaced by "charity." In six of these instances the King James restored the word "love." The passage under consideration is one of the remaining 26, where the REVISED STANDARD uses the only adequate English word, "love."

For one another we are to hold love unfailing, "since love covers a multitude of sins." The passage is apt to create the impression that love makes up for many shortcomings, and if only we have love toward people we may get away with a lot of shortcomings. This, however, is not the meaning of the passage. It does not imply that if we have love in sufficient quantity, it will cover up our failures. It is descriptive rather of our attitude toward other people. We must unfailingly maintain love towards them, because love enables us to overlook their shortcomings. The Greek word translated "cover" means to conceal, as by drawing a cover over. Love, in other words, draws a veil over the sins of others. We know that people are sinners, but we look at them as human beings, rather than at their sins. Over their sins we draw the veil of silence or oblivion.

Lord Lister, whose introduction of antisepsis into surgery brought about such dramatic reduction in postoperative fatality, said in a lecture at Glasgow in 1860 that "the two great requisites for the medical profession" are "a warm, loving heart" and "truth in an earnest spirit." "It is our proud office," he continued, "to tend the fleshly tabernacle of the immortal spirit, and our path, if rightly followed, will be guided by unfettered truth and love unfeigned." This sounds rather like Paul's prescription for all believers: "Speaking the truth in love, we are to grow up in every way into him who is the head, into Christ" (Eph. 4.15).

The relationship of love to healing is more and more apparent. During the First World War army doctors became aware of an elusive curative force to which they gave the name TLC—which means Tender Loving Care. Sympathetic understanding is as important as proper medication in the healing of sin and disease. The Thornleigh Girls' Home, in New South Wales, is an institution for delinquent girls, 14 to 18 years of age. The name intends to convey the idea that, in so far as possible, the atmosphere of a home prevails. There are spacious gardens, flower-filled rooms, and good music. Moreover, Sunday breakfast is served in bed! The belief that somebody loves them enough to provide these conditions inspires the girls to live worthily of this affection.

It is pre-eminently in our own homes where we ought to be surrounded by the kind of love which draws a veil over our shortcomings. One of the Ten Commandments in the Old Testament enjoins upon children obedience to parents: "Honor your father and your mother" (Ex. 20.12). It is significant that the New Testament gives no such blanket command. With a frank reference to the Old Testament law, Ephesians (6.1) says: "Children, obey your parents in the

Lord, for this is right." The patriarchal society required unquestioning obedience on the part of the younger generation, but the Gospel demands that they obey parents only when the will of the parents accords with the mind and purpose of God.

Here probably is the true significance of an often misunderstood proverb. The old adage, found in Proverbs (22.6), runs:

> "Train up a child in the way he should go,
>   and when he is old he will not depart from it."

It does not deny that there may come a time, in adolescent rebellion, when he will depart from it, but it does insist that when he is old enough to know better he will get back on the right track. The real significance of the proverb, however, has to do with the kind of help and guidance which parents ought to provide for their children. Benjamin West, a dominant figure in early American art, tells us that it was his mother's kiss which made him an artist. In a childhood painting of his she discerned a talent that deserved to be encouraged. That is what is meant by training up a child "in the way he should go." The "way he should go" is not the bullheaded parent's opinion of the way he should go. The "way he should go" is, rather, the way of his own inclination, his own gifts, his own native endowments. The wise parent will encourage these.

Retarded intellectual development in children, often attributed to physical factors, may be due to parental failure at this point. At the Judge Baker Guidance Center in Boston, a yearlong study was made of 17 families with retarded children. In every instance the mothers as well as their offspring were found to be suffering from deep emotional illness. Although the mothers appeared to be "functioning within normal limits in the community," they all were disclosed to have an unconscious desire to keep their children from learning, with the result that they placed obstacles in the way of their children's development.

By keeping their children in ignorance, the mothers could perpetuate the children's dependence upon them. Hence the mothers could continue to feel needed. On their part, the children, trained to fear separation from their mothers, soon learned that helpless ignorance was a way of postponing the independence they dreaded. The report might have gone further and dealt with the adjustment in each case between the mother and her husband. It was no doubt because of ill-requited affection there that the mothers came to look to their children for the satisfaction of their emotional needs.

Not content simply to amend the old law regarding parent-child relationships, Paul goes on to add a new commandment for parents: "Fathers, do not provoke your children to anger, but bring them up in the discipline and instruction of the Lord" (Eph. 6.4). In "Alice in Wonderland" there is a little boy of whom Lewis Carroll sings:

> "And beat him when he sneezes
> He only does it to annoy,
> Because he knows it teases."

Sometimes children sneeze to annoy fathers who have provoked them!

Schizophrenic patients studied at Boston State Hospital were all revealed to have come from homes where obedience to Paul's commandment was unknown. The patients grew up in families that provided little emotional security. All confessed that they could not really turn to either parent for emotional nourishment or support. The feeling of being unloved creates "tremendous anxiety, anger, and revengeful, destructive fantasies," the study showed. These, in turn, induce in the child fear of equally destructive retaliation from the parents. Self-preservation becomes a matter of intense anxiety, and repeated disappointments lead to complete breakdown. Fear of mutual destruction becomes crystallized in terms of killing and being killed.

Asthma, hay fever, eczema, and other conditions associated with allergy are often thought to arise out of hostility aroused by parents. A study of 90 children with allergy and 53 without disclosed that 98 per cent of the allergic victims felt themselves rejected by their mothers, while only 24 per cent of the others did. The allergic children were unable to express the anger which they felt toward unloving parents. Dr. Hyman Miller, of Beverly Hills, Calif., described the rejected child as "like a cornered animal," who is unable to give vent to his hostility. Repressed feelings produce inner conflicts which show up in asthma or skin trouble. One allergic child said to the doctor: "When mama says she's going away for a vacation, I get darn mad. I feel like smashing light bulbs. But I can't. I just get sick. Then mama can't leave me."

The National Home for Jewish Children, Denver, Col., was established as a free-of-charge institution to care for underprivileged children suffering from asthma and other chronic afflictions of the upper respiratory system. Within two years, 82 per cent of the patients are able to return home free from symptoms. A remarkable fact, however, is that some get well without treatment of any kind. The asthmatic condition clears up as soon as they get away from their parents. "Many of the young patients," says the director, "require little or no follow-through on a medical basis once they get to Denver. Leaving home seems to act as relief." The theory is that escape from parents who have either rejected the child or been over-protective in their attitude toward it provides the needed release from emotional tensions which have had their effect upon the body. Happy are they who at home are not provoked to anger!

The obligation to surround our brethen with discerning love extends beyond the bounds of home. Hebrews (10.24) says: "let us consider how to stir up one another to love and good works." "If you can love," says Dr. Karl Menninger, "—this is the touchstone. This is the key to all the therapeutic programs of the modern psychiatric hospital; it dominates the staff from director to gardener."

The Menninger Foundation has enlisted the sympathetic aid of the entire community in creating an emotional climate favorable to the recovery of its patients. "The people of Topeka," said Dr. Karl Menninger, "know that most mentally ill patients get well if they are treated right—treated with kindness and patience and love and skill, not only by doctors and nurses and aides and therapists but by the whole community. The people in my town are no longer afraid of patients. They know too many of them ... They discover that love cures people, the ones who receive love and the ones who can give it, too." Who would not want to exercise this love to the full?

36. Love Earnestly

Plotinus, a third century philosopher, followed Plato in emphasizing the existence of the soul in contrast to the existence of bodily things. Higher purifying virtues are needed to help the soul become like God by removing from it as much as possible that which is of the senses. Unification with God comes only when the soul, in an ecstatic state, loses the restraint of the body and has for a time an immediate knowledge of God. The doctrine of Plotinus was called Neoplatonism, and this influenced many Christian philosophies of mysticism. During the middle ages successive steps toward the soul's illumination were described as follows: purgation or purification, illumination, awareness, perfect union or spiritual marriage.

This, however, is an extra-Biblical scheme. The Scripture describes no process for the "flight of the alone to the Alone." Not in solitary mystic rapture but in concern for needy brethren does the Scripture suggest God is most truly to be found. 1 Peter (1.22) suggests that purification of the soul leads, not to ecstatic vision, but to neighborly concern: "Having purified your souls by your obedience to the truth for a sincere love of the brethren, love one another earnestly from the heart."

In early experiments with tranquilizing drugs, one group of patients in a mental hospital received one of the drugs, another group received a placebo, or meaningless prescription. Notable improvement appeared in *both* groups! When asked how a meaningless dosage could improve a mental condition, Dr. Karl Menninger suggested: "maybe it was just because for the first time in years somebody paid some attention to them."

A notable illustration of this is to be found in the Gospel story of Jesus' dealing with Zacchaeus, the "chief tax collector" who climbed a tree to see Jesus when he came to Jericho: "When Jesus came to the place, he looked up and said to him, 'Zacchaeus, make haste and come down; for I must stay at your house today'" (Luke 19.5). This is the only recorded instance of Jesus' inviting himself to a man's home! Since Zacchaeus belonged to a despised class, the people could not understand it: "They all murmured, 'He has gone in to be the guest of a man who is a sinner.'"

But that was enough. That did it. The next item in the story is the right-about-face made by Zacchaeus: "Behold, Lord, the half of my goods I give to the poor; and if I have defrauded any one of anything, I restore it fourfold" (Luke 19.8). So far as the record goes, there was no sermon, no argument, no analysis of the situation—hardly even a lapse of time. Jesus' gracious condescension in deigning to go home with him was the touch of fellowship which Zacchaeus needed. When somebody showed concern for him, that made him over!

Jesus often used this form of therapy. The man born blind was cast out of the synagogue. "Jesus heard that they had cast him out, and having found him" (John 9.35) spoke a saving word. A timid woman "had heard the reports about Jesus, and came up behind him in the crowd and touched his garment. For she said, 'If I touch even his garments, I shall be made well'" (Mark 5.27 f). Even though the crowd was thronging, Jesus singled her out and spoke words of healing, peace, and pardon. Mark (1.40 f) tells how "a leper came to him beseeching him, and kneeling said to him, 'If you will, you can make me clean.' Moved with pity, he stretched out his hand and touched him." Lepers had to keep at a distance from all others, and Jesus' gracious touch was the first feel of fellowship he had known since he fell victim of the disease. "The performance of the most amazing marvels," says Edwin Lewis, "is not to be compared spiritually and morally with the act of one who, in a land where ritual uncleanness was held the direst of crimes, voluntarily touches a 'leper' and speaks with kindness in the presence of a crowd to an 'unclean' woman who publicly confessed to have touched him."

When the Duke of Windsor was Prince of Wales he went to India, then a land of so many untouchables. A member of a higher caste would not pass within two hundred yards of one of these along the road. So gracious was the Prince, however, that a group of the untouchables dared to surround his automobile. When one of their number made a speech in behalf of the sixty million "Unclean," the Prince did an unheard of thing. Says one reporter, "He stood up—stood up for them, the 'worse than dogs,' spoke a few words of kindness, looked them all over slowly and so, with a radiant smile, gave them his salute.

"No sun that had risen in India had witnessed such a sight. As the car started on, moving slowly not to crush them, they went almost mad. And again their eastern tongues clothed their thought. 'Brother—that word was truth that our brothers brought us. Behold, the Light is there indeed! The Light, the glory—on his face!'"

The Indian untouchables have been described as "worse than dogs." It is interesting in this connection to note the effect of love even upon subhuman creatures.

A psychologist who has specialized in treatment of dogs contends that their attitudes and dispositions are determined by the affection which they do or do not receive. "Dogs," he insists, "are like children. They need to be loved and understood if they are to learn good behavior patterns. Repress or abuse a child enough and you have a juvenile delinquent. Inhibit and abuse a dog and he, too, will show his rebellion in bad behavior patterns." Extensive canine acquaintance convinces him of the falsity of the belief that certain breeds are more vicious than others; nor does he believe that there are many individual dogs who are vicious. A dog's disposition, he insists, is made by human beings, and the average dog starts life with a good disposition. If a dog is unmanageable, he believes the owner is usually to blame.

His convictions have been demonstrated on a number of dogs which others considered vicious. From S.P.C.A. kennels he took a dog that had been cruelly treated, his tongue cut in half, his front teeth knocked out. By being taken into the home and treated with the respect that would be shown a member of the family, this dog was converted into a friendly, happy creature. This man's interest in the psychological aspect of dog training began when a neighbor complained that he was tired of whipping his German shepherd dog for going out and killing chickens. By showing affection for the dog, the trainer converted this troublesome creature into a "Seeing Eye" dog. At one time the trainer had in his home eight dogs of eight different breeds. The only thing they all had in common was rejection by their owners. Through affection and understanding these all were transformed into creatures little children could love and trust.

Our nation has been sadly lacking in hospital care for the mentally afflicted, but the erection of bigger and better buildings is not the complete answer. A favorite saying of Dr. Will Menninger, who spends much of his time traveling to interpret to the public the problems of psychiatry, is: "Brains before Bricks." By this he means that greater stress must be placed on obtaining sympathetic assistants who may become trained workers, and striving for cures rather than putting up more buildings simply to provide custodial care.

When a famous New York clinician, Dr. Ernst P. Boas, died after 40 years of professional and public life, an eminent lawyer wrote this tribute: "He was the best family or personal physician I ever knew. He seemed scarcely to need medicine; his personality was curative. I remember once asking him whether he was not going to listen to my heart. 'Not unless you wish me to,' he replied. That was enough for me."

The importance of the personal element in emotional rehabilitation was emphasized by an address delivered to the American Psychiatric Association. Dr. Leo H. Bartemeier, the president that year, said that dependence on scientific mechanisms must not be allowed to do away with the personal relationship between doctor and patient. "Every scientific discovery," he said, "every technological innovation, every new refinement in diagnostic accuracy, every new therapeutic technique, diminishes the personal aspects of medical care." Bad results follow "where enthusiasm for mere technology has taken the place of truly scientific humanism."

Work done in love will have certain characteristics which will prove to be good tests in separating the real healer from the fakers. Characteristic of love is humility."Love is patient and kind; love is not jealous or boastful; it is not arrogant or rude" (1 Cor. 13.4f). The fake healer is apt to claim all the credit for himself.

A doctor has estimated that whenever an act of healing occurs the medical profession may be given perhaps 15 per cent of the credit, with the remaining 85 per cent being attributed to the unseen powers through which God works in His world. One physician, asked about this, said: "I should say that a doctor who claims 15 per cent of the credit has a greatly exaggerated idea of his own importance!" The doctor's 15 per cent—or whatever the proportion—is very important, but he ought not to boast of it. Paul says: "Let him who boasts, boast of the Lord. For it is not the man who commends himself that is accepted" (1 Cor. 1.31; 2 Cor. 10.17, 18).

The founder of the Menninger clinic always regarded himself as one privileged to co-operate with God. He is said to have "started every day of his career by asking that it might be a justification of God's goodness in placing him on earth." His own guiding principles he has formulated in these words: "Man's first responsibility is to God; this responsibility can best be demonstrated by a reverence for life that should make each of God's creatures a humble seeker and learner. Where knowledge is gained it should be shared."

This means also that there must be constant examination and re-examination of successes and failures. The man who relies only upon himself will continue to insist that his own techniques are infallible. The humble servant of others will be always asking: why did one treatment succeed in one case and fail in another that appeared to be quite similar? Was it the therapy that worked in a particular case or was it the therapist? Dr. Karl Menninger repeatedly asks: "What do we *know*? How can we be sure?" The physician dresses the wound or assuages the trauma. It is God who provides the healing.

The Menningers point out that when patients recover under psychiatric treatment, it is the psychiatrist who gives the essential technical guidance and the personal inspiration. But, they insist, he must not delude himself by presuming that apart from the response of the patient and the grace of God, success is impossible. Hence, they add, the chief prayer of a psychiatrist should be, in the words of the 19th Psalm:

> "But who can discern his errors?
> Clear thou me from hidden faults.
> Keep back thy servant also from presumptuous
> sins;
> let them not have dominion over me!
> Then I shall be blameless,
> and innocent of great transgression."
> (Psalm 19.12f).

One of the compulsions of love is to seek out those who need its ministries.

37. Sick and You Visited Me

One of man's earliest questions, "Am I my brother's keeper?" (Gen. 4.9) seems to have received its definitive answer in the words of one who said: "As you did it to one of the least of these my brethren, you did it to me" (Mt. 25.40). The manifestations of this brotherhood were as follows: "I was hungry and you gave me food, I was thirsty and you gave me drink, I was a stranger and you welcomed me, I was naked and you clothed me, I was sick and you visited me, I was in prison and you came to me" (Mt. 25.35f). As in our Lord's time, hunger and illness and crime are often found together.

After studying 1,963 persons living in the New Haven area, Yale University scientists concluded that the incidence of psychosis and neurosis has some connection with the social, economic, and educational features of the environment. Neurosis was more common on the higher level, psychosis on the lower. Schizophrenia in the lowest social stratum was twelve and one-half times as great as on the highest level. Moreover, the treatment received by the two groups was "striking and statistically different." Those on the lower level received only organic treatment, while those on the higher level received psychotherapy or psychoanalysis. Greater marital and family instability was apparent also on the lower levels.

Studies carried out at the Jewish Hospital in Brooklyn indicate that dietary insufficiency on the mother's part may be the initial cause of the congenital malformation known as Mongolism. Vitamin A deficiency in animals caused slow skull growth. Accompanied by normal brain growth, this resulted in overcrowding of the skull and consequent distortion of the brain. Compared with normal children of the same age, Mongoloid children suffered from impaired ability to absorb vitamin A. The tendency to bear harelipped children appears to be inherited, and among women who have borne one such child, the chances are estimated at one in seven that a second child will be similarly affected. It has been observed, however, that most harelipped children are born among the poor. At New York Hospital, 59 women, each of whom had borne a child thus afflicted, were given massive doses of vitamin A and B in the early weeks of their second pregnancy. All bore normal offspring.

A paradox of our society is that slum children who become ill are taken to the wards of our finest hospitals where the best and cleanest of everything is available. So long as the child is well, no one seems to worry very much as to whether it lives in the dirt. Physicians generally take the position that this is not their problem. Solving it would involve concern with political processes for which they do not have time or inclination. At the 1953 meeting of the American College of Physicians, held in Atlantic City, one session was devoted to a panel discussion by five medical authorities on how the public can pay for the excellent medical services science now knows how to provide. Of the 4700 physicians in attendance at the gathering, only 53 attended this session. Dr. Louis H. Baehr, president of the association and medical director of the Health Insurance Plan of Greater New York, declared: "Medicine is now facing serious economic problems. Yet doctors are not interested in talking about social and economic problems."

The Greek physician, Hippocrates, who lived about 400 years before Christ, is revered as the father of medicine. He attempted to place medicine on a scientific basis, separating it from superstition, and his methods of observation are still those of modern clinical practice. The Hippocratic oath, though probably not traceable to him, does represent his ideals. In many modern universities it is administered to graduates in medicine. By it young medical men pledge themselves to practice their "art in uprightness and honor" and to hold in secrecy whatever they "see or hear of the lives of men which is not fitting to be spoken." He is author of the well-known aphorism, "life is short and art is long."

Among the writings attributed to Hippocrates are the Precepts, one of which suggests that the physician who feels the purse before the pulse is unworthy; and that preventive medicine is also a part of each man's responsibility. "Sometimes," said the ancient Greek healer, "give your services for nothing, calling to mind a previous benefaction or present satisfaction. And if there be an opportunity of serving one who is a stranger in financial straits, give full assistance to all such. For where there is love of men, there is also love of the art. For some patients, though conscious that their condition is perilous, recover their health simply through their contentment with the goodness of the physician. And it is well to superintend the sick to make them well, to care for the healthy to keep them well, but also to care for oneself, so as to observe what is seemly."

Serious students of the Scripture, however, have been concerned that this need should be met. Dr. Victor Heiser, who will not be suspected of bias toward orthodox Christianity, points out in his volume, *An American Doctor's Odyssey* (New York; W. W. Norton & Co., 1936), that other religions have been indifferent to dirt and disease. His world tour gave him ample opportunity to observe the effect of religion upon health. In a chapter on leprosy, he states, "Christian religious societies have always interested themselves in caring for lepers and have been virtually the only one. All other religions have, as a rule, held aloof. But sympathy for the afflicted, a Christian tenet, has done much to alleviate the sufferings of these unfortunate people."

He who takes the Scripture seriously must therefore be concerned to make scientific knowledge available to all, and those who want to do God's work in the world must pay attention to the economics of modern medicine. Men are unwilling to be taxed to provide decent medical care for their fellows—but appear quite content to go on paying taxes for hospital, police, and court services necessitated by the absence of adequate treatment for all:

> From slums where foul diseases hid,
> The free winds travel far and wide.
>
> The rich man living on the square,
> Throws wide his windows for the air.
>
> His petted child, with every breath,
> Drinks in the viewless seeds of death.
>
> The rich man, bowed down by his woe,
> Wonders why God should send the blow.
>
> The parson wonders, too, and prays,
> And talks of God's mysterious ways.
>
> But know, O man of high estate,
> You are bound up with the poor man's fate.
>
> The winds that enter at your door
> Have crept across his attic floor;
>
> If you would have all well with you,
> Then must you seek his welfare too.
>
> If even selfishness were wise,
> It would no other life despise.

Society's provision for enabling people to meet disastrous illness has not yet been fairly distributed. Public officials frequently and fervently announce that they are opposed to government medicine, and this has been the theme of addresses by President Eisenhower to members of the medical profession. The fact is, however, that considerable segments of our population have long been beneficiaries of government medicine. Our nation maintains the United States Public Health Service, which operates hospitals in many cities. Treated in these hospitals are seamen of the Merchant Marine, members of the Coast Guard, employees of the Postal Service. The army and navy maintain hospitals for the treatment of military personnel and their families (army hospitals even have maternity wards!), and the Veterans' Administration provides medical care after soldiers and sailors have been separated from the service.

President Eisenhower opposes government medicine, but he has himself been its beneficiary on more than one notable occasion. In 1956 he underwent an operation for ileitis at the Walter Reed Army Hospital. He was in the hospital one day over three weeks. The only charge was $1.05 per day for maintenance, and his total bill came to $23.10. During the same period Mrs. Eisenhower was permitted to stay at the hospital at a daily rate of $1.55, so that her bill was $34.10. Twenty-two days of board, room, and hospital care cost the president and his lady $57.20—less than the grocery bill for two people would have been at home.

Four civilian doctors participated in the operation. If they chose to submit bills, they would be paid out of public funds, as consultants to the Army Surgeon General, at the rate of $50 per day. Bills from these surgeons to civilians would probably have been well over $1000. The army doctors who attended the president were not permitted to submit bills, since they are on salary and their income is the same whether their services are required or not. No one begrudges the President the best medical care, but one wonders how a man who benefits from government medicine to such an extent can oppose similar provision for his humbler fellow-citizens. One man of modest means had to pay $1600 a month to keep his wife in a hospital during a prolonged terminal illness caused by cancer of the brain. He will spend the rest of his life trying to pay the bill.

It is sometimes urged that doctors must be allowed to work on a fee basis, rather than on a fixed salary, because otherwise their incentive would disappear. It can hardly be called complimentary to attribute mercenary motives to the heirs of Hippocrates, and certainly the situation in the U. S. Public Health Service proves that it is not true. A pastor was called to a government hospital early one morning. A seaman was thought to be dying. The pastor found that a young staff doctor had been with the patient all night. "Then you were on night duty?" he asked. "No," said the doctor, "there are some of us who just like to stand by in time of need." The doctor was not motivated by hope of a fee. He was a salaried employee of the Public Health Service, and got exactly the same salary whether he stayed up or went to bed.

A well-known surgeon in the same hospital estimated that his salary was approximately one-fourth of the income he could be making in private practice. "Then why do you keep on in the Public Health Service?" he was asked. There were, he said, several reasons. One was that he did not have to keep books, and send bills. He preferred surgery to book-keeping. Another was that he did not have either to provide for himself the best of equipment or arrange to get along without it. Government hospitals offered the best in labora-tory and other provisions for research, experimentation, and testing. Finally, he not only did not have to mail bills but he did not have to think of collecting enough from his patients so that he could take care of his old age. The Public Health Service assured him a pension—and that relieved him of anxiety about investments, whether in real estate, stocks,

or fruit farms which bring so many of the cares of the world
to other members of the medical profession.

"In nothing," said Cicero, "do men more nearly approach
the gods than in giving health to men." It may be respect-
fully suggested that medical men who labor in the spirit of
this U. S. Public Health Service doctor know something of
the joy and security which parish ministers always have
known. The clergyman does not labor for money. Yet he is
provided a home and a salary and, in these latter years, a
modest pension. Knowing that he cannot become rich, he
renounces the quest for gold and concentrates on the relief
of such needs as he is prepared to meet. The local congrega-
tions of one Protestant denomination, in calling a minister,
sign this form: "In order that you may be free from worldly
cares and avocations, we agree and oblige ourselves to pay
you the sum of ———— to give you the free use of the manse,
and to give you one month's vacation." The assumption here
is that no man can be free until his basic needs are met. The
man who has that security knows the joy of giving himself to
meet his brother's need. This opens new possibilities to the
brother.

38. Door of Hope

The Beatitudes are associated with the teaching of Jesus, and
it is true that no collection of beatitudes is quite so extensive
as that found in Matthew (5.1-12). However, there are beatitudes in other parts of the Scripture. Psalm 84 for example
has three:

> "Blessed are those who dwell in thy house,
>   ever singing thy praise!" (verse 4)

"O Lord of hosts,
   blessed is the man who trusts in thee" (verse 12)

"Blessed are the men whose strength is in thee,
   in whose heart are the highways to Zion.
As they go through the valley of Baca
   they make it a place of springs" (verses 5f).

A young woman, shopping in a department store, asked the clerk where she could obtain a compass. "What kind do you want," asked the clerk, "—the kind that goes places or the kind that goes round in circles?" The man whom God strengthens is not a man who goes round in circles but rather a man who goes places. In his "heart are the highways to Zion." The exile, far from home, thinks with passionate longing of a well-remembered place of worship, and in his mind's eye he keeps open the pilgrim road for the day of his return.

When that day comes, the exhilaration will be such that the hardships of the way will be transfigured:

"As they go through the valley of Baca
   they make it a place of springs."

The exact location of Baca is uncertain. The word may refer to a particular kind of shrub, and in 2 Samuel (5.23) is translated "balsam trees" (the King James has "mulberry trees"). Perhaps the locale derived its name from the trees that grew there, just as we have Elmwood, Chestnut Avenue, or Peachtree street. If the intended reference in the Psalm is to the region mentioned in 2 Samuel, the location could be south of Jerusalem. Balsam trees do grow in arid places, and certainly a comparatively sterile spot is intended. This dry valley will turn out to be "a place of springs." The eager joy of the returning pilgrims will find the region much less forbidding than they had expected.

The word "Baca" has been subject to another interpretation. It closely resembles the Hebrew term for "tears" and in several ancient versions was not transliterated, as in ours, but translated by the word "weeping." The Latin Bible here reads *vallis lacrymosa*. As a result, "vale of tears" has become in European languages a synonym for life itself. This is an unnecessarily gloomy view however, because what the Psalmist has in mind is that the vale of tears can be transfigured into a place of refreshing fountains: "Passing through the valley of weeping they make it a place of springs."

A pastor who has had training at the Menninger clinic reports that the doctors there see in this psalm a standard for psychiatrists: "The patients' pains, queerness, isolation, ineffectiveness, disagreeableness, discouragement, idleness and unhappiness challenge the psychiatrist thus understood to become their friend, guide, protector, helper, and lover" (Humphrey Walz: *The Presbyterian Outlook*, 7/18/55). Some suppose that the valley of Baca is to be identified with the valley of Achor, mentioned in Hosea (2.15). In any case, a similar transformation is there envisioned and God's promise is that He will

"make the valley of Achor a door of hope."

On election night, 1952, former Governor Adlai Stevenson sent to General Eisenhower a telegram congratulating him upon his election to the presidency and concluding with the prayer that "you may make the dale of trouble a door of hope." This is Dr. Moffatt's translation of the Hosea passage: "I will ... make the dale of Trouble a door of hope." The word Achor means trouble—some authorities consider it the root of our English "ache"—and those translators give us its true significance who call it the dale of Trouble. The dale of Trouble is a deep ravine that runs very near to the site of ancient Jericho. After a rain it becomes a foaming torrent, and the waters sometimes rush down so swiftly as to engulf the unwary traveler. Treacherous spots like that are difficult to negotiate, and legend sometimes makes them even more dangerous than they are. It is likely, too, that the wandering tribes of Israel had made their way into the Promised Land through this valley. It was in this valley, also, that Achan had been stoned to death, in penalty for his dishonesty. Altogether, it was a name fraught with unhappy association: "the valley of Trouble"—such a name as Bunyan might have chosen to describe some dark passage the soul must take.

But the prophet hears God saying that the nature of this dread place is to be changed: "I will make the dale of Trouble a door of hope." It had already proved itself that. Difficult as had been their ascent of it, it had proven for the Hebrews the gateway to the land which they had sought for forty years. The prophet, of course, lived at a much later time. Hosea's writings date from the eighth century, B.C. Immoral conduct, dishonest business practices, the worship of false gods had undermined the national foundations. Israel in its weakened condition would be an easy prey to any foreign invader. Hosea compares Israel's conduct toward God to that of an unfaithful wife. She has spurned the love that was rightfully hers. She has purchased a cheap and momentary satisfaction that has already begun to pall. But by her own act she has cut herself off from all that was dear, and she now has not much to look forward to. But to give way to despair was to lose sight of the divine element of forgiveness. Hosea, who perhaps had learned this through his own experience, insists that the husband still loves his wife and is willing to overlook the injury that has been done him.

In terms of national life that means that God will restore Israel's security and again build up her prosperity: "Then will I restore her the vineyards, and make the dale of Trouble a door of hope." It is sound psychology when a married couple have been having trouble between themselves, to insist that they go and revisit the scene of their honeymoon: the memories of those first happy associations will return in an upsurge of affection that may carry them over present difficulties. That is exactly the imagery used by the prophet. God will take his people back to the place by which they had first entered the Holy Land. There he will once again become the nation's "husband." The old relationship will be re-established. And the scene where this occurs will gain new significance and a changed name. Luz was just an obscure Canaanite town until Jacob had his vision there. Then it became Bethel, "House of God." So now this dread spot is no longer to be the dale of trouble but the door of hope.

In this ancient story there is help and encouragement for us all. God is ever dealing with us like that. How often does he cause us to go through the Valley of Affliction until it becomes the Gateway of Opportunity! Daniel Boone is remembered as one of the most famous of American frontiersmen. His career is, in a singular way, bound up with the early expansion of America. Born near Reading, Pa., he went with his parents, at the age of 16, to settle in the Yadkin Valley of North Carolina, from there his exploits took him to western Pennsylvania and Florida. Tales of Kentucky intrigued him and he went on a journey of exploration through the Blue Grass region. After further adventures in Virginia and West Virginia, he wished to settle down in Kentucky. The title to his properties, however, was imperfect and, in spite of his services to the state, he lost them. After his last holding was gone he moved to Missouri, where he received a large grant of land from the Spanish government and was made a district magistrate.

From this period of his life the biographer has preserved some words which indicate how for him fortune had altered.

"Many dark and sleepless nights," he said, "have I spent separated from the cheerful society of men, scorched by the summer's sun and pinched by the winter's cold—an instrument ordained to settle the wilderness. But now the scene has changed." In those few words there is summed up the long history of the Christian church. It, too, has had its dark and sleepless nights, but it has learned that "dark will break to dawn." The church, too, has endured the scorching heat of persecution and the cold winter of indifference. But always there has been a seedtime and a harvest—these have not failed. And in Boone's words also are suggested the circumstances under which one may expect the dale of Trouble to become the door of hope: "an instrument ordained to settle the wilderness." He did not claim credit for his success—he was but "an instrument." He was not self-appointed; he was "ordained" of God for this work. His task was to "settle the wilderness"—that is to say, it was his duty to do everything within his power to bring about the change.

Men compelled to live with disease have found that the dale of Trouble could become the door of hope. Writers' cramp is the affliction ordinarily associated with literary people, but a group of British authors found that they were all afflicted with diabetes. They and others thereupon organized the Diabetic Association and arranged for the publication of a quarterly journal, written for diabetics by diabetics. Hugh Walpole was editor, H. G. Wells and G. D. H. Cole among the contributors. In the first number of the publication, H. G. Wells declared that he had found diabetes "an invigorating diathesis." He thereupon congratulated his fellow-diabetics on their being members of a high and austere cult.

Their characters are strengthened by the daily and perpetual discipline of self-control. They are men who have learned to detest the saccharine in thought, word, and deed. Formerly when a man had diabetes, you waited for him to die. Wells announced that hereafter society should rather look for the diabetic influence in every aspect of life—in art, in science, in conduct. As for himself, he was confident it would manifest itself in a new and delicate strength, marked by clarity and restraint.

Concern for the needs of others may also change the dale of Trouble into the door of hope. In 1915 there were some American missionaries in the Near East who wondered what they, while war was raging, could do to relieve human suffering. They organized a relief expedition. A doctor and a clergyman were at its head. They had four nurses and fifteen medical students. The group arrived just in time to assist in caring for the wounded brought back from the first unsuccessful attack on the Suez Canal. This was the Turkish army to which these Americans were bringing relief. This Christlike act made a profound impression throughout the Near East. "Particularly were Moslems astounded to see foreign Christians going into danger to serve the soldiers of an unfriendly army. Many Moslems who had for years been suspicious of the missionaries gave up their long held antagonism." This brought American influence in that part of the world to a new high.

When Bartholomew Diaz more than four centuries ago rounded the southern tip of the dark continent and saw the turbulent waters he named the place "Cape Troublesome." Later, his more far-seeing sovereign called it "Cape of Good Hope." Was this merely a primitive euphemism, involving the belief that if you gave a dangerous spot a benevolent name it might change its disposition? Perhaps, but it is a parable of Christian experience. They who allow themselves to serve as instruments of Providence are always discovering that Cape Troublesome is really the Cape of Good Hope. This is one of the lessons taught in the school that God conducts.

39. *The School of Suffering*

One of the pointed questions which people used to ask about Jesus was this: "How is it that this man has learning, when he has never studied?" (John 7.15). The issue arose when Jesus went into the temple and presumed to set himself up as a public teacher. According to the standards of the time, he was not qualified to be a teacher. He had not been to the right schools. If any one in Hebrew society wanted to be a teacher, it was the custom that he should go to the rabbinical school and be trained in all the traditions of the race and all the details of the law. Paul boasts of having been "brought up . . . at the feet of Gamaliel" (Acts 22.3).

But Jesus apparently never had an education at all in the conventional sense: "How does this man know anything of books," the people asked, "although he has never been at any of the schools?" It is, of course, possible to be educated without ever having been to school—just as it is possible to have been through school and still not be educated! A young man went to teach in a school in the southern mountains. He had a Bachelor of Arts degree from Princeton University, a Master of Arts from Columbia University, and a Bachelor of Divinity degree from Union Theological Seminary. He had also three full years of teaching experience, having been for that length of time an instructor in the American University of Beirut. He had also spent his summers studying at Geneva, Grenoble, and other places on the continent of Europe.

If any one were qualified to teach in a southern mountain school, it should have been he. But the state officials were not so sure. They were not going to let him teach until he had taken a course at their normal school. In somewhat similar fashion, the officialdom of his day was sure Jesus was not qualified to teach: "How can this man read, when he has never gone to the right school?" There are various answers to the question. Russell Conwell was sure that the greatest university in the whole world was life on a farm, where one grows up in daily contact with elemental forces and becomes aware of his dependence upon the good earth, where the snows of winter shut one in and give him time to think.

Jesus had certainly been to this school. We have but to leaf through the parables to discover how well he had read the book of Nature. The parables remind us, too, that although Jesus may not have been educated in the formal sense, he was nevertheless a complete master of language and literary form. No one has ever equaled his skill at turning out epigrams or relating narratives with "the brief, condensed simplicity of genius." Even those who had been to the right schools recognized this man's exceptional powers: "he taught them as one who had authority, and not as their scribes" (Mt. 7.29).

The Letter to the Hebrews (5.8) gives us a hint about still another school which Jesus had attended—a school of quite a different sort: "Although he was a Son, he learned obedience through what he suffered." Here is the suggestion that Jesus' triumphant life was possible because he had been to the school of suffering, and of what he learned there. There can be no doubt that Jesus carried a very heavy schedule in this school. The New Testament makes it plain that it was no correspondence course which he took, either. He was present daily in the classroom and he studied after hours. Consider at what a youthful age he was enrolled in this school. When he was a tiny babe, the king undertook to slay him, and his family had to flee with him down to Egypt. Here was his pre-kindergarten!

Following his twelfth year, the Gospels make no mention of Joseph, so it is likely that the one who stood to him in the relationship of father died early. Many suppose that the reason Jesus did not enter upon his public career until he was 30 was that he had to support his mother and a large family of brothers and sisters. Here at the carpenter's bench he attended the University of Hard Knocks. Toward the end we also find him at night school: after supper he came out and "went as was his custom, to the Mount of Olives . . . And being in an agony he prayed more earnestly; and his sweat became like great drops of blood falling down upon the ground" (Luke 22.39, 44).

All his life long Jesus had a perfect record for attendance at the school of suffering. He never missed a day. But he learned something: "Although he was a Son, he learned obedience through what he suffered." People ought always to learn something when they suffer, and one of the real ministries of religion is to help people to bear suffering creatively. One of the things we learn when we suffer is how many friends we have. We never know until we are brought low how many there are to help, nor how generous and willing and thoughtful our friends can be. We learn also to appreciate the learning and wisdom of the physician and the skill of the surgeon. We learn a new sense of dependence upon a power not ourselves: the surgeon dresses the wound —it is God who brings healing.

We acquire also a new perspective. Life appears one thing when we are able to rush hither and yon, wherever we wish. It takes on a rather different appearance when God puts us on our backs, that we may look up. We learn sympathy when we suffer—and tolerance of those who are permanently disabled. A certain physician, driven from his profession by tuberculosis, said: "The struggle with tuberculosis has brought me experiences and left me recollections which I never could have known otherwise, and which I would not exchange for the wealth of the Indies."

One reason that Jesus is so universally understood is that through suffering he became fully one with our race. When the author of the Letter to the Hebrews writes "Although he was a Son, yet he learned obedience through what he suffered," there is an implied astonishment that Jesus should have suffered—astonishment perhaps that God's Son should have had to learn anything. Yet the Gospels make it plain that he was so fully one with us that he had to go through all the normal human processes of acquiring knowledge and experience. Had he never gone to the school of suffering, his kinship with us would have been only make-believe. Spiritually he grew in wisdom and in stature and in favor with God and man by what he learned in the school of suffering. All who have tried to deal philosophically with suffering have had him in mind. "Knowledge by suffering entereth," says Mrs. Browning. "Poets by their sufferings grow," said Samuel Butler, and what Shelley says of poets is true of all great creative spirits: "They learn in suffering what they teach in song."

If even Jesus learned obedience by the things which he suffered, we can scarcely hope that it will be otherwise with us. There is no such thing as "Salvation in ten easy lessons." We, too, must learn it the hard way. God still presides over the same school—and there are some basic things in man's education which have not changed. One is that it is still intensely individual and intimately personal. It is something each one has to acquire for himself. When the game of tennis was first introduced into Syria, the well-to-do students could not understand why the Americans would give themselves all that trouble. If the ball had to be knocked back and forth, why didn't they let their servants do it for them?

They didn't understand that physical betterment is something a man must cultivate entirely on his own. Nobody can do it for him. A student visited the magnificent ruins at Petra, perhaps the most amazing monument to an ancient civilization found anywhere on earth, "the rose-red city half as old as time." A certain royal prince was vacationing there. His highness did not bother to go out and inspect the ruins for himself: he sent his secretary to do it for him while he remained comfortably in camp. He had not learned that growth of one's mind is something one has to cultivate for oneself.

So also in the school of suffering. Pain is always intensely personal, and we cannot employ any one else to answer roll-call for us in this school. "To suffer," one has said, "is to be alone; to watch others suffer is to know the barrier that shuts each of us away by himself." The circumstances of our learning have not altered much since the days of Jesus. This is a timeless problem which modern technology seems unable to do anything about. In the year 1934 Admiral Richard E. Byrd spent four and one-half months in solitude near the South Pole, with temperatures outside running as low as 83 degrees below zero. It was not until four years later that the world learned the full story of the intrepid explorer's experiences. He reported that his sufferings were so intense that it took him that long to make up his mind to write about them. He was outfitted as thoroughly as modern science could equip him. He had "a balanced ration, duly fitted out with vitamins, and the means for cooking it." He had chemical heat pads, to warm him in bed. He had a radio set for sending and receiving. But many things went wrong, and we are told that he came as near to dying as any explorer ever did who finally came through. And, says one observer, "dying surrounded by what were meant to be modern conveniences appeared no more pleasant than dying plain."

Technology has not been able to alter—nor even to sugar-coat!—the process of learning. It still remains true, also, that when we enrol in the school of suffering we must choose our teacher well. James A. Garfield said: "Give me a log hut, with only a simple bench, Mark Hopkins on one end and I on the other, and you may have all the buildings, apparatus, and libraries without him." Although some of our colleges have become country clubs, the best means of education is some one who knows. Lewis Mumford points out that the most modern classrooms and "the most luxurious student dormitories will never serve the cause of education as well as the presence of intelligent and courageous professors."

No amount of reading, either, can ever take the place of personal attendance at the school of suffering. Canon Raven reminds us that "language, as any one who has ever tried to write to the newly bereaved must know, is insufficient even when handled with the skill of a poet and the sympathy of a friend: only immediate and living contact, the touch of life upon life, can transmit a true report." In the school of suffering there is one Jesus whom we call Master. It is He who can trace the meanings hidden in adversity. It is He who can teach us to read "the holy hieroglyph of pain."

Jack Peurifoy, onetime U. S. Ambassador to Greece, was killed in an automobile accident while serving as his country's representative in Thailand. Peurifoy's younger son, a normal healthy lad of nine, lost his life in the same accident. Another son, a spastic, survived the crash. During the family's residence in Greece, the crippled son, Clinton, played freely with Queen Frederika's two children, and was a frequent guest at the royal palace.

One day Prince Constantine said to his little American friend: "My sister and I have been talking about you, and we have decided that you must be the favorite pupil of Jesus." "What do you mean?" asked Clint. "Well," replied the prince, "you know how it is. In school the best pupil is always given the hardest problems to solve. God gave you the hardest problem of all, so you must be His favorite pupil."